Keyboarding Skills
for Children
with Disabilities

DOROTHY E PENSO, DIP COT, SROT, FAETC

Senior Paediatric Occupational Therapist
Child Development Centre, York District Hospital

Consulting Editor in Occupational Therapy
CLEPHANE HUME

W

WHURR PUBLISHERS

LONDON

© 1999 Whurr Publishers
First published 1999 by
Whurr Publishers Ltd
19b Compton Terrace, London N1 2UN, England, and
325 Chestnut Street, Philadelphia PA19106, USA

British Library Cataloguing in Publication Data
A catalogue record for this book is available from the
British Library.

ISBN 1 86156 101 6

Printed and bound in the UK by Athenaeum Press Ltd,
Gateshead, Tyne & Wear

Contents

Acknowledgements   vi

Chapter 1   1

Introduction

Chapter 2   7

Children who will benefit from learning keyboarding skills

Chapter 3   26

Assessing the need for learning keyboarding skills

Chapter 4   39

Choosing the most suitable equipment

Chapter 5   62

Methods of teaching keyboarding skills

References   82
Further reading   83
Glossary   85
Useful addresses   89
Appendix: Worksheets   93
Index   217

Acknowledgements

The development of word processing has enhanced the lives of many children who have sensory, motor and/or perceptual problems. It is these children, their parents and their teachers who have helped to shape these methods of learning keyboarding skills. Over the years many therapists have asked me how they can best teach word-processing skills to children with a variety of problems and have urged me to record my ideas.

Acknowledgement is given to P.C.D. Maltron Ltd for permission to publish images of their special keyboards in Figures 4.3, 4.4 and 4.5. ACCO UK Ltd kindly loaned the transparencies which are reproduced in Figures 4.6, 4.7 and 4.8. SEMERC provided the images for Figures 4.1, 4.2, 4.9 and 4.10. The help and co-operation of these three companies is greatly appreciated.

The hands on worksheets 118, 119 and 120 are those of Joanna Penso.

I am grateful for the patience, help and encouragement of my publisher. Throughout, I have had the support of my husband, Giovanni.

Note: In this text 'word processor' refers to the apparatus on which word processing is produced. 'Word processer' refers to the person who operates the word processor.

CHAPTER 1

Introduction

During the past 30 years or so a quiet revolution has been taking place. Typewriters, even electronic ones, have become obsolete. Personal computers and word processors have changed from being expensive pieces of equipment used by only large businesses and certain departments of universities to being readily accessible in every classroom and in an increasing number of homes.

Attitudes towards recording on paper with anything other than a pen or pencil have also changed. Not very long ago parents were devastated should an occupational therapist suggest that their child should learn to use a word processor or personal computer instead of producing all his or her written work with a pen or pencil.

Many teachers believed that there was some innate virtue in using pen and paper to record information, knowledge and ideas. Handwriting was seen as an absolutely essential element in education. In the world of work, handwriting used to be an essential skill in many types of employment. For many people the pen has been completely superseded by computers, computerized equipment and word processors.

Today parents are proud of their child's expertise with computers, which they perceive as the way forward in education and in ensuing careers. Many schools prefer and encourage students to use a word processor for the presentation of assignments and course work.

Children now become familiar with computers during their early years in school. An increasing number of children are born into families in which a personal computer is readily available. Personal computers are, for many, a means of playing arcade and similar games. Computers are a means of accessing information from CD-ROMs as well as the Internet. At secondary school level, information technology (IT) is a subject to be studied to some degree by all students. Some children use a personal computer as a means of studying word processing and other office and accounting skills.

For some children a personal computer can be almost a lifeline should they have difficulty, for any of a number of reasons, with recording information, ideas, knowledge or creativity on paper. The ability to use a computer keyboard efficiently and confidently can revolutionize their educational aspirations, allowing them to access academic courses in ways that were not even dreamed of in the past.

This is not to suggest that only children who have obvious difficulty with handwriting will be helped by learning to use a word processor. There are many reasons for apparent difficulty with handwriting, not all of them involving mechanical difficulties with using a pen. Some people are not verbally adept and have difficulty expressing themselves in spoken language as well as with the written word. A word processor will allow such people time and space to experiment with words and commit to paper only work which they have revised and edited, with which they are completely satisfied. Some people have problems with ordering or sequencing information to record it on paper, while others have severe spelling difficulties which results in frequent corrections and overwriting, leading to a written page which is neither legible nor pleasing to the eye. Word processing will allow spelling and word order to be checked and amended and the completed page to be error free.

This book contains information which will help the reader to decide which children will benefit from learning to use word processing for a proportion of, or all, their work which involves recording on paper. It gives details of the process of assessing the need to learn keyboarding skills. This includes looking at many types of congenital and acquired neurological difficulty, mechanical reasons for limitation of movement, perceptuo-motor difficulties and visual problems, as well as some aspects of reading, spelling and specific handwriting problems.

It would be unwise to suggest specific models of computer, laptop or dedicated word processor, for each model is rapidly superseded by a new model with additional and more advanced facilities. Equipment that was considered 'state of the art' a short time ago quickly becomes dated. It seems likely that this rapid progress in the development of equipment will continue apace for the foreseeable future. For these reasons, features and facilities will be discussed but specific models will not be named. There are, however, examples of specific models of auxiliary equipment, such as keyguards, expanded keyboards, wrist rests and some types of programs.

Some children need to record their school work using a word processor from their earliest days in school. For other children it becomes apparent as they progress through school that handwriting will never be an efficient means of recording on paper. Some children develop normal handwriting skills then at some point during their school years lose those skills, maybe because of a head injury or as a result of brain surgery. For most of these children unorthodox or sometimes custom-devised methods of teaching keyboarding skills will be required.

This is not a book that will help children who have very severe physical difficulties who need to use complex electronic devices and switching systems in order to be able to use a word-processing system. It is a book for helping children to develop their most effective way for using a personal computer or word-processor keyboard. It does not attempt to teach keyboarding skills or word processing to the level required by a professional word processer or secretary. Its aim is to suggest methods by which children who are unable to demonstrate their potential with pen and paper can do so by using their personal most effective means of operating a word processor or personal computer. The level of word-processing skills is limited to those required to produce pieces of work that are well laid out, easy to read and pleasing to the eye.

It is imperative that all children who are to use word processing to record all or part of their school work are taught keyboarding skills so that they are familiar with the position of letter characters on the keyboard. The practice of 'pecking' about the keyboard with one finger should be discouraged and the optimum method of firing keys for each particular child carefully taught. Unless children are taught to use a keyboard to the best of their ability, word processing will be of little use and may be as irksome as handwriting.

This book contains a number of methods of teaching these skills, together with the corresponding keyboarding exercises, set out one to a page for clarity and ease of use. *All the pages of keyboarding exercises are photocopiable.* Some of these exercises are simplified versions of conventional methods of learning keyboarding skills. Others are for children who are able to use only a limited number of fingers or for those who have the use of one hand only.

For children who have impaired vision which is likely to deteriorate, it is of course advisable to teach 'touch-typing' or, more correctly, 'touch word processing', so that there is no reliance on vision when using a word processor. For children with other conditions the acquisition of touch-typing skills does not hold any great advantage. For children who have perceptuo-motor or dyspraxic-type difficulties, attempting to teach touch typing can be counterproductive, as many such children are unable to organize precise finger movements if vision is entirely excluded. The method used to teach keyboarding skills is important and must take into consideration the specific needs of each child. It is important to choose the correct time to introduce keyboarding skills, when the child is receptive and the child's life will not be overloaded with the extra work involved.

The basis of teaching keyboarding skills used in this book is the vertical method as opposed to the more common horizontal method. In the latter method all the fingers are used from the beginning, which is not appropriate for many children with disabilities. The vertical method involves one finger at time, that finger firing vertical rows of keys most of the time. Should only a limited number of fingers be appropriate to use for word processing, this method allows for ready adaptation of fingering. Over many years the fundamentals of the vertical method of learning the keyboard has been found to be most suitable to use and adapt for children who have some difficulty with recording on paper by other methods. It is easy to adapt for one-handed users as well as those who can only use a limited number of fingers.

This book aims to help anyone who is involved with children who have difficulty recording thoughts, information and knowledge by means of pen and paper. It will be useful for therapists, educationalists and the parents and carers of children with disabilities.

Paediatric occupational therapists are usually the health professionals who assess hand function and pen and pencil skills. Often they are closely involved with the child's acquisition of keyboarding skills and in giving advice to teachers and parents. In some instances speech and language therapists treat not only the comprehension and execution of oral language but also treat difficulties with the written word. They may therefore be involved with the use of word processors and computers. It is important that they are aware of the optimum methods of teaching these skills to fulfil the needs of specific children.

Some areas of paediatric occupational therapy and speech and language therapy employ helpers and technicians who are often involved in the acquisition of practical skills such as word processing. These people should be conversant with the principles of teaching keyboarding skills to children.

Today, fewer schools are designated for children with special needs. Of those that remain, it is particularly important that all staff, teachers, pupil support assistants and technical staff are familiar with the methods their pupils use to access keyboards, as well as the teaching method which was or still is being used for each child. An increasing number of children with disabilities are receiving their education in mainstream school. Their teachers and pupil support assistants therefore need to be familiar with methods of teaching keyboarding skills so that there is uniformity of approach.

Should a child be using keyboarding skills at home, parents and carers should know in detail the methods that are being used in schools. It is important that parents and carers are able to help their child to acquire these skills, and to do so they need to be able to make suggestions with confidence.

Lecturers and other staff in colleges and universities involved with education of therapists and teachers will benefit from familiarity with the methods appropriate to the teaching of keyboarding skills to children with any type of special need. They should be aware of those who will benefit from using some form of word processor and the methods of teaching that are likely to be most effective for a particular child. They should be very much aware that the way in which a child uses a keyboard should be the most effective way of recording on paper for that particular child and that the aim is not to produce keyboarding skills commensurate with a secretary or word processor operator.

Staff of colleges and universities who are involved with students who are able to record effectively only when using a word-processing system should all be familiar with necessary techniques and keyboarding systems. They should be aware that the use of a word processor does not necessarily mean that the person will be able to record more swiftly than would be possible with handwriting.

It has been estimated in the Warnock Report (1978) that 20% of children will have special needs with regard to physical, cognitive or behavioural abilities at some time during their school days. It is reasonable to believe that a fair proportion of these children will have some degree of problem with recording on paper using a pen or pencil. Many of these children will be helped by learning keyboarding skills in a manner suited to their specific needs.

CHAPTER 2

Children who will benefit from using keyboarding skills

There are innumerable disabling conditions that can result in handwriting being slow, uncomfortable, painful or requiring continuous conscious effort. The effects of the symptoms of these conditions detract from the amount of concentration, effort and energy available to devote to the content of work recorded on paper.

Recording on paper involves far more than the effort and motor planning required to inscribe words. It also entails knowledge and application of spelling skills, the construction of sentences and paragraphs, and planning complete pieces of work. It often involves the recollection of knowledge and facts, the use of imagination, logic and reasoning. It is therefore vital that every person has at their disposal their most effective and effort-free method of recording on paper so that the necessary attention, concentration and effort may be given to the content of the work. For many people this optimum method of recording on paper will be by means of word processing using a personal computer, laptop computer or dedicated word processor.

The most effective method of learning and using keyboarding skills depends on the nature and severity of a person's difficulties and whether they involve sensory, motor, motor planning and/or perceptual problems.

Instead of detailing the many conditions in which word processing will be the most effective method of recording on paper, the following pages give indications of some of the *symptoms* and *characteristics* that occur in those conditions. Thus the reasons for introducing word processing and how the skills are best taught will become clearer.

Many children have a number of symptoms that do not fit neatly into a particular syndrome. Some have problems that do not provide the means of making a precise diagnosis. Consideration of prevailing symptoms will provide a framework which can be used to choose the most suitable word-processing equipment and introduce the most effective teaching methods.

Symptoms may be part of conditions that are congenital, present since the perinatal period, or acquired, developing after birth. These two main groups of difficulties may each be divided into a number of subgroups defined by the cause or nature of the problems .

Symptoms and characteristics of conditions that occur in childhood

- Sensory symptoms that are related to any of the senses, most usually vision or hearing.
- Perceptual symptoms, which are concerned with processing at a cerebral level or making sense of sensory input.
- Motor symptoms, which are concerned with the response to perceived sensory input, most usually by some form movement.

Sensory input, perception of sensory input and motor response form chains of events that are continually taking place throughout the waking hours. An example of this process is seeing (sensory input) a person in the street, recognizing that person as a colleague (perception) and greeting the person (speech, which is motor output). A further example of this process is a mother hearing (sensory input) a baby's cry, recognizing (perception) the cry as that of her own baby and walking (motor output) to the cot to tend to her baby.

Sensory symptoms and characteristics

Visual problems

Visual acuity, the capacity for seeing distinctly the details of an object, may be impaired. Such problems may be remedied by the use of spectacles. Squint, also known as strabismus, may or may not affect visual acuity.

The visual field is the extent of space in which objects are visible with the eye in a given position. The visual fields may be incomplete. Any area or areas of the visual fields may be affected. In hemiplegia there is often reduction of the left or right visual fields of both eyes. This may result in the child being unaware of visual stimuli on the side of the impairment. Children usually learn to compensate for this deficit with head movements.

Tunnel vision is present when only the central visual fields are intact. Peripheral vision is present when only the areas on the outside edges of the visual fields are intact. In all conditions where there is a visual field deficit, care should be taken to ensure that the child is scanning the whole of the keyboard and that the monitor or visual display unit (VDU) is arranged in the best position for maximum vision.

A very small proportion of the population suffers from complete colour blindness, the inability to appreciate colour. A larger proportion suffer from defective colour vision. Some people find very pale shades difficult to differentiate, while others have difficulty with pink/orange or blue/green discrimination. Care should be taken when using colouring as a teaching aid that the pupil is able to perceive the differences in the colours used.

Some colours and combinations of colours are easier to look at than others. Some children perform measurably better when they are given particular contrasts between foregrounds and backgrounds. Should a child be having problems with foreground/background discrimination, other contrasts should be tried until the best contrast for that child is obtained.

Nystagmus is a condition that occurs in a number of syndromes. It is characterized by repetitive movements of the eye, most usually in a vertical or horizontal direction. People who suffer from this condition usually learn to use the parts of their visual fields where the nystagmus is least troublesome. This may result in the head being held in unusual positions. All these visual problems are likely to have an effect on copying skills, scanning the written or printed page and monitoring the screen of both completed work and work in progress. When selecting word processors and personal computers it is important to consider visual problems. Attention should be given to the position and size of the monitor or VDU as well as to the resolution of the screen, its colour and the contrast between the background and character display.

Hearing impairment

The degree of hearing loss is, of course, variable between a slight loss in one or both ears, and profound loss where speech and other sounds are not heard. The frequencies where hearing is lost also vary. Some have difficulty with low-frequency sounds while others find high-frequency sounds inaudible.

There is a high incidence of hearing impairment in cerebral palsy. There is a strong association between dyskinetic or athetoid cerebral palsy and high-frequency deafness.

Hearing impairment will need special consideration when teaching keyboarding skills because the student will be looking at the keyboard or VDU and not at the teacher. Some students may need to monitor lip movements to be able to interpret speech. In some neurological conditions the noises of involuntary foot movements on wood or vinyl floors can be an additional distraction when attempting to hear speech sounds. The provision of a simple foot rest covered with thick carpet will reduce this source of noise.

Proprioception

This is the appreciation of posture, balance and position by means of receptors, called proprioceptors, within muscles, joints and tendons, and the vestibular apparatus of the inner ear. Children who have problems with proprioception may have difficulty with sitting balance and appreciating the position of body parts without resorting to visual clues. Poor proprioceptive skills are particularly significant in the hands and fingers when word processing.

Insensibility to pain

A small percentage of the population has impaired appreciation of pain. Such people have little or no tactile appreciation of when they have injured themselves. This symptom may occur in isolation or with other symptoms.

Spina bifida is a condition in which there is a lesion of the spinal cord. There is partial or complete loss of sensation, including insensitivity to pain and pressure below the level of the lesion. In practical terms this means that great care must be taken to ensure that there is no damage caused below the level of the lesion by burns or scalds, abrasion or other damage to the skin.

Symptoms and characteristics of impaired perception

Perception is concerned with the ability to process, organize and interpret sensory information from internal and external stimuli. Children who have impaired perception may have difficulties in one or more of the following areas.

- Appreciation of one's own body image. We all have an internal perception of our own size, shape and configuration.
- Appreciation of our own position in space without visually or manually referring to that position.
- Appreciation of our own spatial relationship to other objects and people. Difficulties in this and the above two areas of perception result in incoordination of movements, generally at both a gross and a fine level.
- Visual appreciation of position in space and spatial relationships. Difficulties in these areas may result in problems with reading, spelling and writing. There may be difficulty with differentiating between letter characters of similar shape but different orientations such as 'b' and 'd'.

Difficulty with the relationships of letters to each within words will cause spelling or sequencing problems.

- Figure/background appreciation involves the ability to distinguish the relevant object or figure from a background which may be plain or complex. Usually it applies to vision or hearing. Some children have difficulty concentrating on, for example, a teacher's voice particularly when there is background noise. Similarly children may be unable to concentrate on the task in hand when in a classroom that has lots of pictures on the walls, equipment on tables and shelves, and children moving within the room. Such children cope best when their word-processing monitor has a very simple layout free from unnecessary icons and devices.

Perceptuo-motor difficulties

This group of difficulties is characterized by poor motor skills at both a gross and fine level. There may be difficulties with planning, organization and grading of movements. There are often problems with balance, rhythm and proprioception. There may be difficulty with various aspects of perception, such as visual discrimination, visual spatial skills, visual memory for single forms, and sequential memory, completeness and closure. These visual problems may be manifested as purely visual difficulties or they may also be associated with motor activity in life situations. Some people have problems only with perception applied to life situations, such as judging speed and distance of vehicles when planning to cross a road.

These difficulties have been known by a variety of names; in recent years both 'motor learning difficulties' and 'developmental co-ordination disorder' have been used. In earlier times the terms used were less kind, and included 'congenitally maladroit' and 'awkwardness of movement'. An overview of the history of these difficulties is provided by Hulme and Lord (1986).

Dyslexia

A percentage of the population has a greater or lesser degree of difficulty with the written word, which is the literal meaning of 'dyslexia', i.e. *dys*, difficulty with, and *lexia*, the written word. There may be difficulty with reading, spelling and handwriting Word processing can help because it removes the need to recall and reproduce the complex pen movements needed for letter character construction. It is necessary only to recognize and locate letters on the keyboard. Because editing facilities are infinite, the student can produce acceptable work wherein correct spelling and sentence construction is reinforced. It has been estimated that between 1% and 3% of the population have some degree of dyslexia (Springer and Deutsch 1989).

Asperger's syndrome

This condition is considered to be on the autistic spectrum and a pervasive developmental disorder. It affects the development of a number of abilities, many of them of a social nature. The main symptoms are intense fascination with certain subjects, such as train timetables or makes of cars. Often actual verbal communication is poor with formal use of language, which can be repetitive. (One mother described her son as having developed language skills as if he had been learning a foreign language.) People with Asperger's syndrome find it difficult to develop friendships because of problems interpreting body language and facial gesture. Attempts at interactions with other people are often inappropriate and one-sided. For example, a young boy turned to the man next to him in the bus queue, who was a complete stranger, and said, 'Are you the fat controller?' He was, of course, alluding to one of the characters from *Thomas the Tank Engine*. Often 'conversations' are completely one-sided and inappropriate, being simply an outpouring of factual information on the current topic of obsession.

Many people who suffer from Asperger's syndrome have co-ordination difficulties at both a gross and fine level and have particular difficulty with the production of legible and even handwriting. As Tony Attwood (1998) discusses in his book *Asperger's syndrome: a guide for parents and professionals*, this handwriting difficulty can cause embarrassment and anger. Many people who are affected by this syndrome are especially skilled with the use of computers and word processors. The use of such a device can greatly enhance school life and, with special permission, enable examination papers to be completed efficiently and legibly.

Attention deficit disorder and attention deficit hyperactivity disorder

Attention deficit disorder (ADD) can occur as a problem of attention or it may also include hyperactivity or overactivity, when it is described as attention deficit hyperactivity disorder (ADHD). Children with these disorders have difficulty taking part in interactive play – although they want very much to play with other children, they do so badly. They can be destructive, both in specific peer interaction and in general classroom and home situations. They have short concentration spans, which may vary according to the activity and the circumstances in which it is undertaken. There is usually a high degree of distractibility and impulsivity. ADD and ADHD can occur with other conditions, such as cerebral palsy, dyspraxia and Asperger's syndrome.

Word processing and the use of a monitor or VDU can help to increase the concentration span and decrease distractibility by providing a focus for attention and a medium with which the child can perform at a level commensurate with his or her peers.

Epilepsy

All those who teach or treat children who have epilepsy should be aware of the likelihood of seizures and know how to act in the event of one occurring. For a minority of children with photosenitive epilepsy there is a possibility of bright computer screens precipitating seizures (Hosking 1982). Medical advice should be sought if photosensitive seizures are thought to be a possibility.

Emotional and behavioural problems

The problems may occur in isolation, with other, physical, symptoms or they may be the result of frustration and poor self-esteem caused by physical symptoms. The teaching of keyboarding skills may require exercises devised specifically for a particular child and measures may be required to stimulate motivation and concentration. When the child has acquired keyboarding skills and no longer has great difficulty recording on paper, there may be a reduction in behavioural problems as frustration is reduced and self-esteem increases.

Case note

Nicholas has mild athetoid cerebral palsy. During his days in the infant department of school his hand skills were sufficient to allow him to draw effectively. In fact at this stage he was quite a star, adding interesting and often very amusing detail to his pictures. He was able to write at a level commensurate with his peers, though had he not had impairment of hand function he would have had very superior skills, especially with the content of his work. His reading skills were very much above average.

By the time he entered the junior department of his school at the age of 7, his frustration was beginning to show. He had neither the motor skills nor the speed necessary for him to record on paper to demonstrate his obviously superior intellectual level and to satisfy his own aspirations. His frustration soon became obvious, as he developed behavioural problems and became defiant and disruptive in class. His head teacher consulted his occupational therapist who had been treating him since his pre-school days. It was decided to introduce him to a keyboard and teach him the necessary skills to become proficient with its use. He was a more than willing student and though he was able to use only the index finger of each hand and his thumbs for the space bar, within a year he had attained a speed of 25 words per minute. His head teacher was amazed not only with his progress with his keyboard, but also with the dramatic improvement in his behaviour in the classroom.

Symptoms and characteristics that affect motor activity

This area may be divided into two parts, motor or movement planning and actual movement.

Motor planning

This is the planning or organization of movement at a cerebral level. Difficulty in this area is known as dyspraxia. The complete inability to plan or organize motor tasks is known as apraxia.

True dyspraxia can cause great difficulty with the acquisition of handwriting skills. Children with dyspraxia will usually have no difficulty with movements *per se* but will have great difficulty organizing movements. The difficulty may be developmental and resolve with increasing maturity or it may persist into adult life. Dyspraxia is not concerned with the ability to perform movements, nor with perceptual skills, it is concerned with the *planning* of movements and sequencing of movements at a cerebral level.

There may be associated difficulties with concentration and remaining 'on task'. There may be behavioural and/or emotional problems.

Symptoms that affect movement

These symptoms may be divided into several categories.

- Neurological, concerned with the function or dysfunction of some part of the nervous system.
- Limitation of movement, which may be caused by joint malformation or dysfunction, swelling or pain.
- Trauma to nerves, bones, muscles or other soft tissue, which is likely to affect movement.
- Congenital malformations to any body tissue which affect movement.

Neurological

Ataxia

Ataxia is characterized by a coarse tremor which affects the head, trunk and limbs. There is an intention tremor of the hands which will preclude all but the briefest items of recording with pen or pencil. Ataxia may be a symptom of cerebral palsy or acquired as a result of head injury. It is unlikely that swift and legible handwriting will develop, therefore keyboarding skills should be taught at the earliest opportunity.

Friedreich's ataxia is a progressive disease characterized by increasing ataxia, nystagmus and kypho-scoliosis. It manifests itself in the early years, often with such symptoms as 'clumsiness' or incoordination, and initially may be treated as such. Handwriting will become increasingly laboured and eventually completely impractical.

A personal computer may be used for writing and also for other skills which are usually undertaken with pencils and crayons, such as artwork, illustrating projects, graphs and diagrams. Suitable programs may also be introduced to facilitate progress in number, word and other educational concepts. Depending on the severity of the ataxia it may be necessary to introduce a keyguard or in some instances an expanded keyboard to help to avoid mis-keying which ataxia can cause.

Athetosis

Athetosis is characterized by involuntary, slow writhing movements. In some children there are also quick, jerky movements which are called chorea. The condition is usually apparent during the first months of life, when there is marked developmental delay and retention of reflexes after the age at which they have disappeared in the average child. Most children will not develop useful handwriting skills. Some will be able to use a regular keyboard, perhaps with the addition of a keyguard. Other will require expanded keyboard or even sophisticated switching devices to record on paper.

Hemiplegia

This may be congenital, as in hemiplegic cerebral palsy, or acquired following head injury or cerebrovascular accident. Usually the arm is more severely affected than the leg. The human hand is required to perform finer, more precise and complex tasks than the foot. The most precise of these tasks is probably handwriting, where not only the actual movements are complex but the motor planning at a cerebral level is also of a complex and constantly changing nature. This is particularly significant when the hemiplegia affects the innately preferred hand, for the person will then be using what would have been the non-preferred hand for precise tasks such as handwriting. There may also be other complications in that many of those who have severe movement difficulties on their hemiplegic side may also have minor motor problems on the opposite side, which will be apparent only when undertaking complex fine motor tasks such as handwriting. There may a further difficulty when undertaking handwriting with the unaffected hand. As periods spent handwriting become more prolonged there may be increased tone and involuntary movement in the affected side which, for some children, can be a distressing distraction which also causes discomfort and even pain.

Word processing is often the most realistic method of recording on paper for many children with hemiplegia. Careful planning will be required. Where the hemiplegia is comparatively mild, the affected hand may be used to fire the shift key, space bar and other keys on the periphery of the keyboard. Where this is possible, it can be used to help maintain a symmetrical position. When the hemiplegia is severe, one-handed use of the keyboard will be the realistic proposition using a conventional or specially arranged keyboard. Special attention will need to be given to maintaining a symmetrical overall position when only one hand is operating the keyboard.

Diplegia

This occurs in one of the earliest types of cerebral palsy to be described in the middle of the 19th century by Dr William Little. Occasionally it is still referred to as Little's disease. It is characterized by increased tone in the hamstring and adductor muscles of the legs which causes sitting, walking and balance to be delayed. The development of ankle, knee and hip contractures is common, though physiotherapy regimens will help to prevent the development and reduce the severity of contractures which may already be apparent. Care should be taken when planning the seating to be used for word processing to ensure that contractures and spasm is not increased by inappropriate seating provision. Where flexion of the hips to 90 degrees is difficult, a foam rubber wedge may be used, with the highest part of the wedge at the back of the seat. This will enable the hips to be less flexed and thus the sitting position will be more comfortable because there will be less strain on the hamstring muscles at the back of the leg.

Cerebral diplegia is characterized by spasm and contracture in the lower limbs but frequently there is some involvement of the upper limbs, which may be apparent only when very precise activities such as handwriting are undertaken. A large percentage of people with cerebral diplegia benefit from learning keyboarding skills so that their slight but significant upper limb involvement is minimized by removing the need to produce large quantities of handwritten work. This will be especially helpful during secondary school years when projects, assignments and other pieces of work will be required. Usually it will be best to use a pen for brief activities that require recording on paper, and word processing for longer pieces of work.

Before word processors were in general use, Christie Nolan painstakingly typed, with his mother's help, two books (Nolan 1981, 1987). Christie suffers from severe cerebral palsy and for many years could communicate with only a very few people who could understand the meaning of his eye movements. His books, one poetry and the other an autobiographical novel, illustrate the nature of this condition far more elegantly than any medical textbook. He describes the day on which the head teacher of a mainstream school accepted him as a pupil. He describes his joy by saying simply, 'I levitated', which describes so elegantly both his elation and the grossly abnormal movement caused by his cerebral palsy. Christopher has recently published his third book.

Drooling

It is often difficult for children with neurological conditions to establish automatic control of drooling or dribbling saliva from the mouth. They often have poor lip closure because of poor muscle tone so that saliva readily escapes from the mouth. They are frequently unable to undertake more than one task at a time, so that a child who may be able to control drooling when concentrating only on that task, may not be able to do so when also using a computer keyboard. Therefore the continued concentration necessary when using a keyboard may cause excessive drooling and it may be necessary to fit a plastic glove or skin to protect the keyboard.

Tremor

> *Each of us has a normal physiological tremor which is almost imperceptible to the naked eye. The frequency of the oscillations of physiological tremor varies with age from 6 cycles per second before 9 years to 10 cycles per second at 16 years, the frequency begins to decline after 40 years until it has returned to 6 cycles per second at 70 years.* (Fahn 1972)

Abnormal tremor may be a symptom of several conditions, including cerebral palsy.

Benign essential tremor may affect several members of the same family. For example, it is known in one particular family to have affected a father, his twin daughters and the son of one of these twins. This type of tremor will not be observable in infancy but only at the stage when fine and precise manual tasks are attempted. Benign essential tremor sometimes persists when the limbs are at rest, but the amplitude always increases with muscle tension and involves most particularly the hands and fingers. Clearly this will affect all fine motor skills and perhaps most importantly the ability to write without undue effort as well as legibly and evenly. The use of a word processor is usually the preferred method of recording on paper for people so affected. This is not to suggest that handwriting will never be used. It is advisible that keyboarding skills are taught early before the child feels frustrated by lack of speed and progress with the quality of handwriting.

Dystonia

This describes the symptom of slow writhing movements which affect the muscles. This symptom occurs in some types of cerebral palsy. There are also several specific syndromes of dystonia including dystonia, musculorum deformans.

> *Dystonia musculorum deformans ... is a disease of the basal ganglia characterised by strong sustained twisting and writhing motions of the somatic muscles. Any muscles may be involved in these involuntary movements, but most often the muscles of the trunk and the limb girdles are affected producing torsion of the limbs and the vertebral column.* (Johnson et al. 1962)

One of the symptoms of the syndrome is that the dystonia becomes more pronounced when another person is observing an activity being undertaken. This can erroneously be construed as the sufferer intentionally exaggerating symptoms, which is definitely not the case. Diagnosis can be difficult because of the nature of dystonia.

Lack of muscle power

Muscle weakness or lack of power occurs in a number of conditions, including those listed below.

- Duchenne muscular dystrophy, a form which affects males. Usually the child needs a wheelchair by his early teen years and hand function becomes progressively more impaired.
- Becker muscular dystrophy is another form which affects males but the symptoms are less severe than in the Duchenne type.
- Limb girdle dystrophy affects both males and females. The rate of progression of symptoms is variable but is usually relatively slow.
- Spinal muscular atrophy occurs in several forms. The main feature, in addition to muscle weakness, is contractures around the joints.

Further information about these conditions can be found in *An Introduction to Paediatric Neurology* (Hosking 1982) and *The Child with Disabling Illness* (Downey and Low 1982).

Keyboarding skills should be taught well before handwriting becomes difficult or impossible. This will enable the transition from handwriting to word processing to be planned with the least possible psychological trauma. When choosing seating and devices such as wrist or hand support, care should be taken to ensure that appropriate support and positioning is provided for the trunk and limbs.

Limitation of movement

Movement may be limited by a number of symptoms including inflammation, swelling, pain and scar tissue. There are a number of conditions in which these symptoms occur. Some of these are described below.

Juvenile chronic arthritis (JCA) is not a single disease but a whole group of conditions which affect the joints of children and young people.

> *The definition of JCA is that there must have been an arthritis of at least 3 months' duration, starting before the 16th birthday with the exclusion of other diseases that could mimic the condition.* (Craft 1985)

JCA may affect a small number of joints (pauciarticular) or many joints (poliarticular). There may be only one episode of active disease or it may wax and wane throughout childhood. Inflammation and swelling of the hands and wrists may preclude handwriting for periods of time. In JCA it is not advisable for joints to be sustained in the same position or for repeated pressure be applied to them, making handwriting inadvisable, particularly when the disease is active. Often a keyboard with the addition of a wrist rest is the best method of recording on paper. See also *Management of juvenile chronic arthritis* (Griffiths and Craft 1988).

Scleroderma is a condition in which there are flexion deformities with tight, waxy skin. It may begin to develop in the hands and face and may then spread throughout the body. These flexion deformities of the hands may preclude handwriting or make it an impractical means of recording all but the smallest amounts on paper. Keyboarding skills may be adapted to suit the specific flexion deformities that develop.

Morquio syndrome is one of a group of disorders of metabolism of complex sugars known as mucopolysaccharides (MPS). Lax ligaments affect many joints and are particularly significant in the joints of the legs, shoulders and wrists. Many children and young people who have Morquio syndrome will find handwriting fatiguing and impractical for extended pieces of work. When introducing word processing it is important to consider spinal abnormalities when arranging seating. (See also Penso 1992).

Burns and other hand injuries may require the application of dressings or casts which preclude handwriting. It may be possible to undertake word processing using both hands or only the uninjured hand. This can enable the student to maintain work recorded on paper and thus avoid interrupting progress in school during long periods of incapacity of the preferred hand.

Arthrogryposis is a disorder of the connective tissue which encapsulates skeletal joints. It results in varying degrees of limitation of range of movement of joints, fixation of joints in extension, flexion and other more complex positions. Few or many joints may be affected. The condition may occur on its own or with other conditions, such as spinal muscular atrophy or partial limb deficiency. Keyboarding skills are usually of great benefit to these children for both word processing and accessing other educational and leisure computer programs.

Osteogenesis imperfecta is more commonly described as 'brittle bones'. A slight fall or even a movement can result in a fracture which may be difficult to heal. These children often lead sheltered lives and their movements are restricted. Deformities often ensue and these children tend to be of extremely small stature. Equipment with a small keyboard may be indicated to avoid unnecessary arm, hand and finger movements.

Achondroplasia is a condition in which the epiphyses of the long bones unite at an early stage of development, resulting in the characteristic short limbs. In some types of achondroplasia there is arthritic pain which can, over the years, become severe. Usually the hands are broad with very short fingers, which may result in handwriting being slow and requiring more than usual effort.

Syndactylism is a condition in which there is webbing or fusion of the fingers and/or toes. The degree of webbing or fusion varies between slight webbing at the base of two fingers to all the fingers, and sometimes the nails, being fused together. It may be possible to divide some or all of the fused fingers surgically. These symptoms occur in Apert's syndrome (see Jones 1988). Word processing may be the most effective method of recording on paper for people with syndactylism, but methods of using the keyboard may have to be adapted to suit each hand, and high speeds may never be attained.

Partial or complete limb deficiency

There are a number of rare syndromes in which there is partial or complete upper limb deficiency. When one upper limb is intact, handwriting will usually develop well. Should the limb that is partially or completely absent be the one that would have been dominant, then handwriting with the other hand may not become swift, even and legible. Word processing will then be a useful skill, especially for long pieces of work.

Amniotic bands which develop *in utero* may result in deformity or amputation of what would have been the distal parts of limbs.

> *Partial to complete ring-like constrictions occur as a rare anomaly*
> *of the limbs and very rarely the head. At times fibrous-appearing*
> *bands have been noted at the sites of constriction, sometimes having*
> *a broken strand connected to the amnion proper.* (Jones 1988)

Sometimes the deformity or amputation involves the forearm or more commonly the fingers.

CHAPTER 3

Assessing the need for learning keyboarding skills

It will be apparent from an early age that some children will never acquire efficient handwriting skills because their hand function is severely delayed or deviant. Other children will begin to learn handwriting, and only when they are required to produce quantities of writing at speed will it become apparent that they will never attain the required speed. An injury that occurs or disease that develops after efficient handwriting skills have been attained may result in handwriting ceasing to be a useful means of recording on paper.

Careful assessment of hand function and other skills will help to determine the usefulness of word processing, the most suitable types of equipment and the most appropriate teaching methods. Assessment may be divided into four parts:

- neurological
- limitations of movement
- vision
- educational level and skills.

The following should also be considered when the introducing word processing:

- the environment in which the word processor will be used
- the opinions of the child concerned
- the opinions of the child's parents or carers
- the attitudes of the staff in the school the child attends.

Assessment is not a single event that occurs at one time and holds good for all time. Assessment is taking place against a background of a child who is at a certain stage of development and will continue to develop and change until he or she reaches maturity. Many children with disabilities continue to make developmental progress beyond the age at which maturity is usually reached. Very few disabilities remain absolutely constant; they change in their nature, decrease and sometimes increase in their effect.

Neurological assessment

Medical information will already have been gathered about many children whom it is thought would benefit from learning keyboarding skills. Discussions between medical and paramedical staff together with those involved with the educational process will provide a further pool of information and opinion about the child in question.

Whatever the medical diagnosis of a particular child, it cannot be presumed that the symptoms which are relevant in one child with that diagnosis will be equally relevant in another child with a similar diagnosis. For example, three children may be diagnosed as suffering from athetoid cerebral palsy.

- The most significant symptom for the first child may be athetosis which results in erratic movements at both a gross and a fine motor level.
- For the second child high-frequency deafness which is often associated with athetoid cerebral palsy may create the biggest problem. It may prevent the child hearing what the teacher wishes to be recorded on paper. Deafness may impede or even preclude peer relationships. The noises created by involuntary athetoid movements may further interfere with hearing.
- The third child's barrier to learning may be behavioural problems which have developed as a result of difficulty in coping with physical symptoms.

Therefore it can be unwise to draw conclusions about a child's needs exclusively from a medical diagnosis. The prevailing symptoms are of much more significance when devising plans of how best to help a child.

Stability

Before considering how children will be able to use their hands on the keyboard and even before considering general mobility, overall stability should be assessed. To assess stability, consider normal child development and how control and stability is attained. *The Development of the Infant and Young Child* (Illingworth 1983) and *From Birth to Five Years* (Sheridan 1975) both provide excellent accounts of child development.

Children who do not develop stability of the head, neck and trunk, and especially of the shoulder and pelvic girdle, will have difficulty maintaining a stable sitting position and may require seating specifically adapted to their needs. These difficulties will have effects on the ease with which a word processor may be used.

Considerations for children who do not have fully developed stability include the following.

- Children who lack stability will need to use concentration and effort to maintain their position. They are likely to tire easily with the effort of maintaining their position and consequently have less energy, motivation and effort available for the task in hand. It is important that these children are seated in a position that provides them with the necessary support to enable them to direct all their efforts and concentration towards the task in hand. Advice should be sought, most usually from the child's occupational therapist and physiotherapist, regarding suitable furniture and any other support that may be needed to leave the child free to concentrate on the acquisition of keyboarding skills.
- Head control is important to allow the eyes to be used effectively and to facilitate hand/eye co-ordination. It is important that equipment, including

- the monitor/VDU, is placed so that the head can be suitably positioned.
- Where necessary, the trunk should be supported so that during word processing activities the child can give his or her full attention to the task in hand. Clearly such children will need to work towards improving trunk control; however, it should be practised as a separate activity and not combined with this or other precise motor tasks. Support, as advised by a physiotherapist or occupational therapist, should be used whenever the child is working on hand skills. The trunk, and more particularly the shoulder girdle, must be stable in order to support the arm, which in turn must support the hand. The hand must be supported in a suitable position for firing the keys. It is important to appreciate the relationship of stability of the trunk and upper limbs when undertaking manual tasks.
- Stability of the pelvis is part of a good sitting position. Children who have poor pelvic stability will also have difficulty, when lying in a supine position, to make a bridge supported by the feet and shoulders with the pelvis raised from the floor. Where there is doubt about stability of the pelvis advice should be sought from an appropriate therapist, who will probably already know the child well and be aware of devices that have helped with stability of the pelvic girdle while undertaking other manual skills.

Mobility

Many children who have neurological problems and/or developmental delay may progress towards independent mobility at a slower rate than the average child. Some of these children will also demonstrate a deviant pattern of development in that this pattern will not be in the sequence followed by most children and may contain elements which are not part of normal development. The most common stage to be omitted is crawling.

Whatever the early pattern of a child's development it can be difficult, if not unwise, to attempt to predict future attainment. Some children develop skills which, during the early years of life, would not have been predicted. Others set out full of promise but unfortunately do not reach their expected potential. Some children may never attain a level of independent walking that will be a useful life skill. That is not to say that such children will not attain an alternative means of mobility. Mobility by means of a wheelchair can be, for some, more useful and realistic than walking.

Factors affecting mobility

- Neurological and mechanical difficulties may preclude walking completely or allow only very limited walking.
- A change in the texture of the floor, for example from vinyl to carpet, can affect walking ability. A child who is able to walk indoors may find the slight changes in level, unevenness of surfaces, grass, pebbles and the like, very difficult to manage.
- Inclines or downward slopes can add to walking difficulties. An incline can cause difficulties for children who have tight tendo calcaneum, because the incline means that the foot needs increased dorsi-flexion, i.e. the angle at the ankle will be less than 90 degrees. Similarly, the propulsion of a manually operated wheelchair will require more power on an upward slope and more control on a downward one.
- Mobility, either by means of wheelchair or walking, can be affected by the presence of other people. Those who have balance difficulties and those who must give their full attention to the process of walking will find moving within a crowded environment daunting or even impossible. Children who have visual perceptual difficulties will find that weaving their way between their peers who are moving quickly, erratically and unpredictably, very difficult. They will have problems anticipating the moves of others as well as judging their speed and their distance from each other and from themselves. These situations affect some children who use either a manual or powered wheelchair; they may not be efficient with control of the chair or may have visual perceptual difficulties which make

their judgement of width and distances inaccurate.

- Mobility issues are relevant to children who use word processing as a means of recording on paper, particularly at secondary school level, where each subject may be taught in a different classroom. At this stage a laptop is the most usual type of machine to use because of its portability. Even a machine that weighs perhaps a couple of kilograms can be difficult to manage for a child who has mobility problems. A child who uses a wheelchair will need a safe place to stow their machine while in transit between lessons.

- Stairs are a further hazard for those with walking difficulties. They may be negotiated with care when the child in question is alone or with a support assistant. It may not be possible to use stairs when other children are also present. It may not be possible to negotiate stairs *and* carry a laptop. Obviously those who use a wheelchair will need the use of a through floor or stair lift. The latter will require a staircase of sufficient width to accommodate the track of the lift without it becoming a hazard for other children using the staircase.

Mobility, therefore, does affect the choice and situation of word-processing equipment. It should be an element in assessment during primary and secondary school days and plans should include considerations for further education and the world of work.

Fine motor skills

Hand skills begin to develop from a very early age. In the early months grasp is crude, but in normal development it becomes refined and hand skills develop into many precise and sophisticated movements and sequences of movement. *The Development of the Infant and Young Child* (Illingworth 1983) and *From Birth to Five Years* (Sheridan 1975) both provide details of the development of hand function.

Symptoms that may limit hand function

Does the child have one or more of the following symptoms? These symptoms were described in Chapter 2 as symptoms of various conditions. Many of them will preclude handwriting partially or totally. Word-processing skills are highly desirable for children with any of the following symptoms:

- ataxia
- spasticity
- athetosis
- dystonia
- hypotonia
- tremor
- dyspraxia
- pain/swelling
- joint laxity/hyperextensibility
- limb/digit deficit
- syndactylism
- lack of full range of joint movement.

Taking into consideration any of the above symptoms that may be present, and the child's developmental level compared with the normal range, it should be possible to answer the following questions with regard to word processing.

- Will the child be able to use both hands? Does the child already use both hands for play and other activities?
- Will only one hand be used? Will it be the left or the right hand?
- Can some or all of the fingers function individually? Can the child place the hands palm down on a table or other surface and raise each finger separately? With the hands in the same position can the child tap with each finger individually?
- Will it be possible to use all the fingers?

These answers will help to decide the following:

- exactly how the child will be taught word processing
- the approximate speed it will be possible to attain
- the type of equipment which will be most suitable.

Vision

It has been estimated that 40% of the brain and its input is devoted to vision. It follows, therefore, that those children who suffer brain damage of any kind are likely to suffer from some disorder of visual function. Visual skills are usually needed during the acquisition of keyboarding skills and while using them. Assessment should include the following.

- Measures of visual acuity.
- Estimates of the extent of the visual fields.
- Colour contrasts which are best for the child. Does the child need a strong contrast between foreground and background material? Are there combinations of contrasts which the child can see more easily than others. These details are important for both the contrast between the keys and the colours in which the characters are printed on them and the background colour contrasted with the print colour of the monitor.
- Other visual anomalies that will affect the use of a personal computer or laptop. These will include problems such as nystagmus and amblyopia.

Children should have these areas of visual skills assessed by an orthoptist and/or ophthalmologist, as appropriate, and their findings should be taken into full consideration when choosing equipment and methods of teaching keyboarding skills. It is important to appreciate that *how* vision is used is frequently of greater significance than the precise level of visual acuity.

Educational levels and skills

For word processing to be meaningful, the representation of words on paper must have some meaning. Children who have not reached this level will be best introduced to a computer keyboard with other, appropriate, programs.

Learning keyboarding skills should be allied to educational level and where possible, especially with younger children, integrated with the reading and spelling curriculum. How keyboarding skills are taught will be planned after discussion with teachers, pupil support assistants, special educational needs co-ordinators, educational psychologists and others who have active involvement with the child, such as special advisers for children with hearing or visual impairment.

The aim should be to acquire keyboarding skills which will allow the child to record on paper at least at the same level as their peers who have no such difficulties with using a pen or pencil. This target may not always be attained because some children who are unable to undertake handwriting may also be unable to attain high speeds of word processing. Examples include children who have a degree of unsteadiness for any of a number of reasons, those with severe dyspraxia and some children with limitation of movement. However, word processing is still a valuable skill even if high speeds will never be attained. It will provide the child with a means of recording on paper which requires far less motor control, less power and more simple motor planning and organization than does handwriting.

Concentration

Some children with conditions such as hyperactivity and/or attention deficit disorder will have difficulty with concentration in many situations. Children who suffer from either or both of these conditions, often in addition to other disorders as diverse as dyspraxia and cerebral palsy, will have had expert diagnosis by a child psychiatry team. For many such children the ease with which words can be recorded together with the clear display on the monitor can aid concentration on the task being undertaken.

Motivation

Children who have had a handwriting career of constant failure and disappointment understandably have poor motivation. Keyboarding skills can be used to increase motivation by increasing successful situations, presenting a constant clear image of words to reinforce spelling skills. For children with a low level of motivation it is important to choose teaching methods that bring swift results by incorporating words and phrases with keyboarding exercises as early as possible.

The overall assessment of children's strengths and needs will lead to an informed choice of word-processing equipment and teaching methods. To be thorough and look at all aspects of skills required to use a word processor, the assessment will be intra-disciplinary and include the expertise of educationalists, medical practitioners and the therapeutic team. The educationalists will include first and most importantly, the class teacher, as well as the head teacher, special needs co-ordinator, pupil support assistant, educational advisers and educational psychologist. Medical practitioners could include the general practitioner (family doctor), paediatrician and other medical specialists. The therapeutic team will comprise some or all of the following: occupational therapist, orthoptist, speech and language therapist, physiotherapist and clinical psychologist.

Children and parents or carers

This account of assessing children's needs with regard to word processing has, to this point, concentrated on the opinions and expertise of professionals. The opinions of the subjects of assessment – children – and their parents is of paramount importance.

The reasons for teaching keyboarding skills should be discussed with children at a level commensurate with their understanding. The following points should be included in the discussion.

- Underlying abilities which may not be apparent when using a pen or pencil.
- How word processing will help to demonstrate skills which currently are not possible with a pen.
- The fact that, for many children, keyboarding skills will be practised alongside continuing pen and pencil skill practice.
- How keyboarding skills will be taught.
- How equipment will be introduced into the classroom.
- The fact that there will be no pressure to introduce the equipment for classwork until the child feels comfortable in doing so.
- The fact that acquiring keyboarding skills will require effort and application for both the child and the person teaching those skills.

Parents will usually welcome the opportunity to discuss the reasons for their child learning keyboarding skills, what this will entail, and how they may help and support their child. Some or all of the following points may cause concern to parents .

- 'Are you suggesting that my child will never learn to write?' 'Never' can be a dangerous word to use. Some children who during their early years seem very unlikely to develop the necessary fine motor skills and motor planning to facilitate handwriting do manage a certain amount of reasonable handwriting. However, if at the time of assessment a child seems unlikely to develop the skills necessary for handwriting it is usually best to say so in the kindest way possible. If it is thought that word processing will always be required for prolonged periods of recording on paper, this too should be discussed with parents.

- 'I don't want my child to be different.' The fact is that a child using a personal computer, dedicated word processor or laptop will be using a different method of recording on paper from his or her peer group, who will see him or her using this different method. Should a child not be able to record on paper using a pen or pencil at the same level as his or her peers, he or she will also be perceived as being 'different'. When children are able to demonstrate their skills, imagination and knowledge at their optimum level by means of word processing, it is suggested that the 'difference' between them and their peers will be reduced to an acceptable level. The 'difference' between the child and the peer group will, in fact, be less than when the child is producing unacceptable work with a pen or pencil.

- 'Will my child have to use a word processor for "written" examinations?' For some children this will be the best option, though it would not be wise to make such a prediction when a child is very young, for difficulties and abilities change over the years. With older children for whom it is expected that word processing will be the best method for completing examination papers, permission must be sought from the appropriate examination boards. This should be done well before the dates of the examinations. At present if a word processor is used this fact is recorded on the examination certificate. Usually this is not of any great significance with regard to future education or employment. These views should be carefully explained to parents so that they too will have a positive view towards their child learning word-processing skills.

Word processing is surely here to stay. Electronic mail will be used by an increasing number of people in the world of work. Very few people use handwriting to any great extent during paid employment. The handwritten word is used less in private life. Communication is largely by telephone; few personal letters are written. Printed cards are available for almost every occasion and situation. The average person scribbles a note or message for other members of the household or makes a list of items to be purchased. These points may need to be discussed with some parents so that they can appreciate that rather than their child using a word processor being unusual, it is quickly becoming the norm for an increasing number of the population.

Following this comprehensive assessment it should be relatively simple to choose equipment appropriate for the child and the environment in which it will be used. It should also be possible to tailor teaching methods to the needs of the individual child and the level of literacy that has been reached.

Table 3.1 shows examples of the periods of time and the extent of the use of word processing. When a child is assessed as being able to benefit from using word-processing skills, steps should be taken to provide the most effective method of acquiring these skills together with the provision of the most appropriate equipment.

Table 3.1: Examples of the use of word processing

Specific limited times
    Recovery period following brain injury
    Periods of pain, swelling and inflammation during acute phases of juvenile chronic arthritis and similar conditions
    Where there is developmental delay, until fine hand skills and praxis are sufficiently developed to allow swift and legible handwriting
    Periods of time following injury or surgery to the hand

Combination of word-processing and handwriting
    Where handwriting continues to require conscious effort and full attention cannot be given to the content of work
    Where there is lack of power, and fatigue ensues with the effort of handwriting, e.g. muscular dystrophy
    Where short periods of handwriting are possible but the quality of the handwriting deteriorates and/or there is discomfort when the period of handwriting is prolonged
    Some achondroplasias
    Mild cerebral palsy

Word-processing for all recording on paper
    Where handwriting is not a realistic expectation, e.g. moderate to severe cerebral palsy
    In severe degenerative muscular and neurological conditions. e.g. spinal muscular atrophy and Friedreich's ataxia
    Severe arthrogryposis

CHAPTER 4

Choosing the most suitable equipment

Personal computers, laptops and dedicated word processors continue to develop and progress at a rapid rate. Each year, if not each month, further advances are heralded and new software becomes available. It would not be wise to describe or recommend specific items of equipment as such state-of-the art equipment rapidly becomes obsolete. Recommendations are therefore limited to types of equipment, its characteristics and facilities, and processes which should be considered to suit the particular needs of a child. The equipment, which should be chosen with care, includes the items that form the word-processing unit and adaptations that enable children to activate equipment and minimize any manual difficulties which may be present:

- keyboards
- keyguards
- rests for arms and wrists
- keyboard gloves
- visual display unit (VDU) or monitor.

Keyboards

There are a number of characteristics that should to be considered when selecting the most appropriate keyboard for a child:

- overall size
- the angle and 'dishing' of the keyboard
- the qualities of the keys.

Keyboard size

Most personal computers have a standard size of keyboard, which is approximately 45 × 16 cm. The part of the keyboard directly involved with word processing is about 30 × 12 cm. The keyboards of dedicated word processors may be slightly smaller, while laptops may have an even smaller display of keys. The size of the keyboard may be reduced because the keys are smaller than average keys or because they are arranged more closely together, or both these characteristics may apply. So-called palmtop personal computers are now available which, as the name implies, are very small and have proportionately small keys arranged quite closely together.

The size of the keyboard will not be important for some children who intend to use word processing as a means of recording on paper. But for others it will be vital to select the appropriate size of keyboard.

- Hands that lack muscle power are usually most comfortable and efficient when using a smaller size of keyboard so that the distances the hands and fingers need to move is minimized. Smaller keyboards are available on some laptop and palmtop equipment. There is a compact keyboard available which measures 28 cm × 13 cm which is suitable for use with PCs and Acorn A7000 (Figure 4.1). Children who have muscular dystrophy and similar conditions will usually be helped by using one of these smaller types of keyboard.
- Where there is instability, such as occurs in some types of cerebral palsy, the dystonias and ataxias, a larger keyboard layout will usually be best. Some children may require additional devices to prevent misfiring of the keys. There is a large, simplified keyboard available with keys measuring 2.5 cm^2, which is four times the size of conventional keys (Figure 4.2). The keyboard has letter characters, numerals and arrow keys only. There is a version with coloured keys, which is suitable for younger children, and one with conventional white keys.

Figure 4.1 A small light keyboard which measures only 28 cm × 13 cm. It would be ideal for users with limited hand movements or for one-handed users who have particularly small hands. It does not include a keypad.

Figure 4.2 A keyboard with keys measuring 2.5 cm². It contains only letter characters, numerals and arrow keys. It is supplied with lower case stickers. It would be helpful for children with physical disabilities, cognitive or general educational problems. Two versions are available, one has bright, primary colours, and the other is white, which would be more suitable for older children.

- Children with very large hands, broad fingers or syndactylism will find very small keyboards with proportionately small keys difficult to use. For children of secondary school age, where portability is necessary, there may be some conflict between finding equipment of suitable small size and light weight which also has a keyboard suitable to be used by the larger, broader hand.

The angle and dishing of the keyboard

On most standard-sized keyboards there is a degree of 'dishing' from back to front, with the back or side furthest from the user being higher than the front. The degree of dishing varies between manufacturers. This dishing makes the keyboard more comfortable to use, with the fingers in a less flexed position than would be the case if the keyboard was flat. Some keyboards have small extendible supports underneath the back corners which enables the slope of the keyboard to be further increased. Some laptops have no or very little dishing of the keyboard.

The slope of the keyboard can be increased if necessary by supporting it on a sloping surface, such as a home-made wooden wedge which is of a slightly larger size than the keyboard. Sloping surfaces primarily intended as a surface for handwriting are suitable. The keyboard will be more secure on such a surface if Dycem, the non-slip material, is used between the it and the keyboard. A similar effect may be obtained by coating the sloping surface with a rubber solution which is allowed to become completely dry before placing the keyboard upon it. It is also possible to incorporate a wrist or arm support into the construction of a custom-made wedge. This type of adaptation can be of great help to many children; however, it would be cumbersome for a child at secondary school level to transport between classrooms.

The qualities of the keys

It is important that the surfaces of the keys are concave so as to accommodate the fingertips comfortably. This is usually not a problem with the standard size of keyboard but some smaller keyboards have a flat key surface which is less comfortable to use and may, for some, cause difficulties with the accurate firing of the desired keys.

The keys should be of an appropriate size for the fingers firing them, though standard keyboards are suitable for most fingers. Attention should be given to the amount of vertical and horizontal space between the keys, especially where the hand is unsteady and there is difficulty positioning and maintaining the position of the fingers.

Some one-handed typists with a small hand may benefit from using a smaller size of keyboard so that the position of the hand can more easily be adjusted to use all the keys.

It is wise to check that the user can 'feel' when a key has been fired. When word processing, there is an unconscious sensation that keys have been fired. Should this sensation not occur it can be very disconcerting and disturb the flow of work, with frequent checks being made to ensure that keys have actually fired. Today this problem occurs less frequently and usually only with the smaller and less expensive keyboards.

Children who have little power in their finger movements benefit from keys which are fired with little effort. Most keys will fire for a second time and many more times if sustained pressure is applied. Those who have difficulty in quickly releasing pressure from a key that has fired benefit from the word-processing program being adjusted so that the repeat mechanism is not activated so quickly.

Expanded keyboards

Children who have difficulty with the control of fine finger movements, which may be caused by spasticity, athetosis, dystonia or tremor, may find a larger-than-normal keyboard with perhaps larger-than-average keys, and those keys more widely spaced than on the standard keyboard, easier to use (Figure 4.3). They are also available with a keyguard. Expanded keyboards are, at present, expensive, especially when considered in addition to the other items that will be required. However, for some children an expanded keyboard makes the difference between being able to use a word processor and not being able to use one, in which case the additional expense is justifiable. Again there is the problem that large pieces of equipment are not readily transportable between different class or lecture rooms.

Ergonomic keyboards

There are keyboards which are designed to be more comfortable to use than the conventional model (Figure 4.4). They are said to prevent the hand, wrist and arm strain sometimes associated with the conventional keyboard. Some of these keyboards have the usual QWERTY arrangement, while others have an arrangement of keys which place the most frequently used ones in the centre of the keyboard. (The QWERTY arrangement has been used since manual typewriters were first produced. When the typist hit a key it activated a metal rod at the end of which was an embossed character. The character struck the platen round which the typing paper was wound. In front of the platen the inked typing ribbon was held and thus the letter was imprinted on the paper. This procedure was repeated for every character required. The rods with the characters were arranged so that letters which were frequently used in sequence within a word were not placed next to each other, thus preventing the rods becoming tangled.)

So-called ergonomically arranged keyboards have the keys arranged so that the arms of the user are maintained at approximately a shoulder width apart. A rest for the palm of the hand is integrated into the design. There are also ergonomic keyboards arranged to suit people who can use only one hand (Figure 4.5). Both left- and right-handed models are available. These keyboards are currently rather expensive to purchase, though one manufacturer will hire out keyboards on a week's trial so that prospective users may have 'hands-on' experience before making a purchase.

Figure 4.3 An expanded keyboard which would be helpful for children who have unsteadiness or tremor in the hands. It is a made of steel with a wipe-clean nylon coating to withstand heavy use. Note that the construction of this keyboard has the effect of a keyguard because the user needs to place the fingers into the recesses to fire the keys.

Figure 4.4 An ergonomic keyboard with the keys so arranged that the hands and arms are approximately a shoulder width apart. The shape of the keyboard helps to maintain the hands and wrists in a strain-free position.

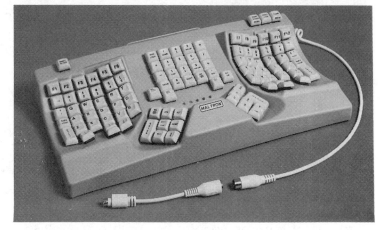

Dvorak keyboards

Conventional keyboards are available for two-handed or right- or left-handed users with the keys arranged so that the most frequently used characters are more accessible. These layouts are available on a Microsoft Access DOS disk.

Figure 4.5 An ergonomic keyboard with the keys arranged to be used by one hand. Models are available for either left- or right-handed users.

This disk also includes information about the following utilities:

- provision for single-fingered use with SHIFT, CONTROL, etc., key combinations
- prevention of extra characters being typed if a key is accidentally fired for a second time
- control of the mouse pointer by using the keyboard
- allows unneeded utilities to be turned off
- adjustment of the rate at which a character is repeated when the key is held down.

Further information about these utilities is available from Microsoft Product Support Services.

Keyguards

If a child has difficulty controlling the finger movements needed to fire the desired key, a keyguard may help to reduce or eliminate the problem. Keyguards are formed from a sheet of either rigid plastic or metal the same size as the keyboard over which it will be used. There are finger-sized holes punched in the keyguard to correspond with the positions of the keys on the keyboard. The keyguard stands a few millimetres proud of the keys so that the finger is placed in the hole to fire the desired key. The keyguard is usually attached to the keyboard with Velcro, with small nuts and bolts, or it fits completely over the keyboard depending on the design. As the size of the keyboard varies between models and types, as does the arrangement of the keys other than the letter characters and numerals, it is important to ensure that an appropriate keyguard is ordered (see Figure 4.3).

Keyguards are intended to be used by people who have quite severe difficulty with accurate firing of keys. Because the finger needs to be placed within a hole in the keyguard to fire a key, and be removed from the hole when the key has been fired, the process is perforce rather slow and great speeds will never be attained. However, for a person who constantly miskeys, the addition of a keyguard will increase accuracy and outweigh the loss of speed.

Keyguards are very helpful for the hand with spasticity, athetosis, tremor, dystonia or limitation of movement. They are also helpful where there is lack of muscle power or any type of instability, because the hand may be rested on and slid across the keyguard as necessary. As the keyguard is positioned slightly proud of the keys, the child using it may need to be seated in a slightly higher position so that the view of the keys is not impaired. Care should be taken to provide appropriately positioned lighting so that the keyguard does not cast a shadow on the keys.

Some children are overwhelmed by the complete array of the keyboard. There may be difficulty dissuading some children from persisting in 'trying' inappropriate keys! A keyguard can be used to display only a limited number of keys. It is easy to obscure all but the required keys by covering the appropriate holes in the keyguard with card secured with tape. Thus the selection of letters which are visible can be changed almost instantly, as required.

Arm rests and wrist rests

Some children benefit from having some support at either wrist level or along the whole length of the forearm. Such support may be advisable because of instability, neurological deficit or lack of muscle power in conditions such as muscular dystrophy. There are many commercially available rests; some are inexpensive, while others, manufactured from more costly materials and of more complex design, are more expensive. Rests for use with keyboards are normal pieces of office equipment and are therefore available from both office equipment stores and computer shops (Figures 4.6–4.8).

It is not always necessary to make a specific purchase if, for example, a large beanbag or a foam-covered block will suffice. Sometimes a book or shallow box of the same depth as the keyboard, placed immediately in front of it, is the best and most simple solution. With all such devices the overall sitting position in relation to the keyboard is very important. The optimum sitting position should be obtained prior to adding any other devices. This usually involves the child sitting at such a height that his or her feet are flat on the floor or other surface, such as a foot rest, when appropriate. The ankle, knee and hip joints should be at approximately 90 degrees. The height of the surface on which the keyboard is placed should allow the elbows to be at 90 degrees and the wrists

Figure 4.6 A simple wrist rest which has a smooth surface and is angled to support the wrist in a relaxed position.

Figure 4.7 A padded wrist rest which is fabric-covered and on a non-slip base.

Figure 4.8 A wrist rest which has adjustable height. It has a lip which slides under the keyboard to keep the wrist rest in position.

to be in mid-position between flexion and extension. A wrist or forearm rest will help to maintain the elbows and wrists in this position. It will also help to prevent strain on these joints in conditions such as JCA.

Keyboard gloves or skins

Keyboard gloves or skins are clear covers for keyboards which closely fit the keyboard's contours (Figure 4.9). The keyboard is used with the glove or skin in place, which is helpful if the child using it has a problem with drooling. Some children with neurological problems have difficulty swallowing excess saliva. The unconscious and automatic swallowing of saliva may never have developed. The problem is often increased because most fine tasks require eye co-ordination, which involves the head being bent forward. This posture, combined with difficulty in swallowing saliva at regular intervals and poor lip closure caused by low muscle tone, exacerbates the drooling problem. Neurological deficits in conditions such as cerebral palsy or dyspraxia cause problems with undertaking simultaneous tasks; thus it may not be possible to use a keyboard while at the same time planning the muscle movements necessary to swallow saliva.

A temporary keyboard glove can be made by covering the keyboard with plastic film intended for covering food. This is, of course, a short-term solution but it may be effective where an immediate solution is necessary. The child using the keyboard covered with film should be closely supervised at all times to ensure that he or she does not tear off the film and put it in or over the mouth.

Figure 4.9 A keyboard glove or skin which prevents liquids from damaging the keyboard. It is a useful addition for children who have a problem with drooling. It does not obscure the keyboard or impede its use.

Lower-case letters

Some children may be familiar with lower-case letters only and find the display of upper-case letter characters on the keys confusing. For this comparatively small number of children it is advisable to cover the upper-case letters with stickers which have the appropriate lower-case letter displayed.

Lower-case letters may be useful in the early stages of learning keyboarding skills, especially if the child is in the early stages of attaining literacy. The stickers may be attached to only those keys that the child will be using, to draw attention to them. Two colours of sticker may also be used, one colour for the keys which should be fired with the fingers of one hand and a different colour for keys to be fired with the fingers of the other hand. I find it useful to use red stickers on the left (port) side of the keyboard and green stickers on the right (starboard). Before embarking on these colour-coding devices it must, of course, be ascertained that the child does not have any colour blindness and that the colours chosen are not those affected by the particular type of colour-blindness that may be present. Stickers may be home-made, though sets of lower case stickers are commercially available.

There is a keyboard available which is supplied with lower-case letter characters on the keys (Figure 4.10). It is suitable for use with a PC, Acorn A7000 and Risc PC.

Judith Stansfield (1997) suggests using a keyboard sleeve as a surface to which lower-case letters may be attached, should this be necessary. This suggestion would be particularly helpful if one keyboard is shared by several children, not all of whom need lower-case letters.

The monitor or visual display unit

The visual display units (VDUs) of the word-processing systems currently available vary from a single line on some simple, dedicated word processors, to a

Figure 4.10 A keyboard which has lower-case letter characters. It would be a useful purchase for a school where a number of children may have difficulty using keyboard with capital or upper-case letters

few lines, to almost a full 'page' visible at one time. The quality of the display is variable and depends on the type, size and quality of the equipment. The following characteristics should be considered:

- size
- resolution
- size of letter characters
- contrast
- angle.

The size of the VDU

This can be an important factor when choosing systems for some children. A full-size display is easiest to work with and for many children helps to concentrate their attention and keep them on-task. Where a number of lines can be viewed at one time it is easy to review and edit text. Should children have difficulty with figure/background discrimination it is possible, on a full-size screen, to display the text with double or even wider spacing to facilitate visual concentration on the appropriate line.

The size of the VDU is only one of many considerations when choosing equipment and sometimes compromises have to be made. For instance, on smaller, portable machines the VDU is usually not so large. On some portable systems the total inner surface of the hinged lid that covers the keyboard houses the VDU. Obviously this is the largest display area possible on equipment of this size. The problem is that these are often the more expensive systems which may be out of the financial reach of many schools and families. VDUs on other systems vary between half a full-size display and a single line showing as few as 25 characters. As a general rule the younger the child or the less academic progress the child has made, the larger the VDU the child will need. Usually small word processors with a very small display are unsuitable for young children. Because so few letter characters are visible at one time it is possible to see only the very shortest complete sentence. Some children become confused by characters disappearing at the left side of the display as new ones are added on the right.

Resolution

The clarity of the visual display is important, and particularly so for children who have visual difficulties. Clarity will depend on 'resolution', i.e. the number of lines on the screen. The greater the number of lines the clearer the display. Parents sometimes enquire if it is possible to use a domestic television screen. It is possible, but the resolution will be much poorer than that of a dedicated VDU and will therefore produce a far less distinct image.

Contrast

The contrast between the background colour and the foreground characters can help or hinder vision. Characters are usually displayed in black or white. The background may be grey, white or a colour. As a general rule the greater the contrast between background and foreground the easier it will be to read the text on the screen. There are, however, exceptions to this rule. Some children are able to cope with some colours and contrasts better than others. If there is doubt about colour suitability the child's orthoptist or ophthalmologist should be consulted and arrangements should be made for the child to test screens of various colours and various contrasts between the background and the characters.

Size of letter characters

This can be important for those with impaired visual acuity and for very young children. Word-processing programs devised for children usually have a choice of character size. The sophisticated programs used with personal computers usually have an infinitely variable character size. It is usually only the very small, simple word processors that are limited in terms of character size. A few machines will display larger characters than they will print. Where character size is important, this feature should be investigated before making a choice of word-processing system.

Most equipment today provides a printout of text which looks exactly the same as the text seen on the VDU – this is known as WYSIWYG, 'what you see is what you get'. There are a few types of equipment that do not have this facility. For example, some programs display a maximum of 40 characters per line on the VDU but will print up to 80 characters per line when the paper is in 'portrait' orientation. Both the word processing program and the printer facilities will need to be checked to ensure that the print displayed on both the monitor and the printed page is suitable for the needs of the child.

The angle of the visual display

This can be crucial to some children. Ideally the child should be able to look directly ahead and see the display. The exceptions to this rule are where the child has limited fields of vision or nystagmus.

The visual fields may be limited in a number of ways, including tunnel vision, where only the central parts of the visual fields may be used. The visual fields may be reduced so that only peripheral vision is possible. In hemiplegia, a condition known as hemianopia may exist where only the right or left half of the fields of vision of both eyes is available. Children whose fields of vision are limited in any of these ways will hold their head in the position which gives them their optimum level of vision. Such children may therefore appear not to be looking directly at the VDU. The advice of an orthoptist or ophthalmologist should be sought if there is doubt about the position in which the head is held and its relation to visual problems.

On some small word processors the VDU may be small and presented in an almost horizontal plane. For some this may not create a problem, but for others the sustained extreme downward gaze necessary to scan the words being typed will be very uncomfortable. This problem occurs in neurological conditions involving the extra-pyramidal tracts. The difficulty can in part be reduced by adjusting the angle of the equipment so that the visual display is presented mid-way between the vertical and horizontal. A small portable machine may be placed on a sloping board, the exact angle of which is calculated to suit the individual child. This will be appropriate only if the adjusted position also places the keyboard in a comfortable position for the child's hand function.

The angle of the VDU will also affect how sunlight or artificial light falls on the display. Care should be taken to ensure that the work area is adequately lit and that the source of light does not cause glare on the screen. Some screens with poor contrast between background and foreground can be seen clearly only when the user is absolutely aligned with the display. This characteristic can create difficulties for the person working with the child because only one person can be in a good position to see the VDU easily. Such displays will be easier to see if a light is arranged to provide vertical illumination on to the screen. Lighting is relatively easy to set up where the word-processing equipment remains in the same position, but can be more difficult where pupils move to a different room for each lesson.

Case study

Sonia was 14 years old with high academic ability when a tumour was diagnosed in the posterior part of her brain. Her post-operative recovery was predictably slow during the first few months. Initially, treatment concentrated on gross movements, stability and mobility. Expressive language was absent for some time. Later Sonia was able to describe the horror of having no means of verbal expression.

Some months later plans were made for a home teacher to see Sonia prior to a very gradual reintegration into school. At this stage her difficulties included unsteadiness when walking, particularly outside the house and on uneven surfaces such as paving stones. She had ataxia in her hand movements which precluded handwriting for recording on paper. Her executive speech was improving though it still lacked rhythm and intonation. She continued to suffer from diplopia or double vision. She was advised that this was likely to be a permanent symptom.

Her occupational therapist advised that in the foreseeable future she would not attain handwriting skills which would be useful in school. She would need a laptop computer which would be easily portable between classrooms. Because of her visual problems she would need the largest possible VDU with the optimum contrast (for her) between the background and the characters displayed. Initially she was supplied with a small word processor which had a very small display set at an almost horizontal angle with very poor contrast between the characters and the background. This was entirely unsuitable because, in addition to her visual problems, Sonia is a tall, slim girl so the proportions of the machine caused her to sit with a very round back in order to see the visual display. In addition her arms were in a very awkward position with her wrists inappropriately flexed.

Eventually it was agreed that she should have a sophisticated laptop computer with a VDU the full size of the machine. The contrast was ideal for Sonia, white characters against a bright blue background. (As an extra it also had a voice-activated word processing program as an emergency backup.) The correct equipment made a world of difference. She was able to use the machine sitting in a relaxed position with her arms and hands optimally placed. She was able to look ahead, instead of down, to the VDU. With the best equipment Sonia was able to work at her highest level and seems set to gain good results in her forthcoming examinations.

Printers

A personal computer system usually includes a compatible printer in the system, as do dedicated word processors. Small laptops do not have an integral printer. Usually material is stored on the hard disk or on a floppy disk and the laptop is then connected to a compatible printer. The availability of a compatible printer should be considered carefully.

Children need a hard copy of their work to hand in to their teacher for marking. In most schools it is important that it is available to the teacher at the prescribed time. In secondary schools work may be required by a different teacher for each subject studied, thus complicating the need for having all work printed at the correct time. If the child has a pupil support assistant (PSA) this should be easy to arrange, but ideally children should be responsible for printing out their own work. This means that the printer should be readily available for the child to use. Very often printers in the information technology (IT) department are not suitable because the room will be open to children only when a teacher is present. The time when the child will be free to print out work will usually be during breaks and lunchtime when supervised use of the IT room will not be possible.

Sometimes the printer used with the personal computer in the classroom will be available. If it is the only system used by a whole class of children it would be unreasonable to expect the printer to be constantly available for the use of one child. Ideally there should be a printer available for the sole use of the child who needs to record on paper by means of word processing. In the case of the child who has mobility problems this becomes particularly important.

Most children, especially as they progress through their secondary school years, are expected to do a proportion of their work at home. For the child using word processing it is important to have a compatible printer available at home. It is possible to take work to school on disk and produce a printout there. In practice, this frequently creates problems as the child will arrive at school anxious to print out work in time to give it in to their teacher at the same time as their peers. The child will also be anxious lest printing out their work makes them late for registration. Some children have been known to abandon word processing and return to producing inferior work with a pen because of problems with producing printouts. A compatible printer at home can often prevent these problems arising.

Portability

In primary school, where children usually spent most of their day in one classroom with one class teacher, the question of portability of equipment rarely arises. It is at secondary school level, where each lesson requires children to move to a different classroom, that it becomes important. For equipment to be truly portable it must be capable of being carried with ease by the user. Some machines are portable in that they could be carried to a car or other vehicle and transported to the place required; this is not true portability. Children moving to perhaps seven different rooms during the day will be carrying their word processor to and from at least seven destinations. Not only will they be carrying a word processor but also the other books and equipment required throughout the day. All this will be carried while other children, many of whom do not always give due regard to children with special needs, are moving around the school. Only the lightest laptops are suitable in this situation. Some children with mobility problems are able to walk reasonably well when other people are not moving in their vicinity. Others find that walking *and* carrying equipment is not possible, while for some, changes in the nature or level of walking surfaces can be a problem. Difficulty with balance can make negotiating stairs a problem, especially when carrying equipment.

Many dedicated word processors and laptops may be powered from the mains supply of electricity or by batteries. Equipment that stays in the same position in the same room can easily be powered from a mains socket, provided a suitable one is available. Where children are moving to different rooms throughout the day, battery-powered equipment is more convenient. Battery power removes the need to hunt for an electric socket in each room. It removes the need for the child using the word processor to sit in what may be an ill-lit and otherwise unsuitable position because it is the only position where an electric socket is available. Perhaps most important of all is the fact that children using a small battery-operated laptop will be able to remain with their peer group.

Batteries do have some disadvantages in that charged ones must always be available, either new or recharged. Some children will need adult help to ensure that the word processor is serviceable throughout the school day. For children of secondary school age, on balance, equipment that can be battery operated is preferable.

Compatibility with other equipment used in school or at home

Equipment provided for a specific child should be compatible with the other computing equipment in the school the child attends. Compatibility makes it easier to organize suitable printers. It also means that information stored on disk can be used with other machines. The same principles apply to equipment purchased for home use, where it is best if parents consult with the school so that there is compatibility between the equipment used at home and in school.

Word processing programs

For many children a standard, commercially available program will be suitable. The program can be set up for the child and he or she then accesses only those facilities of the program that they need to use. Many children become adept at handling such programs and their proficiency helps to boost self-confidence and the esteem in which they are held by their peers.

A number of simple word-processing and desktop publishing programs have been devised specifically for schoolchildren. Often the size of the letter characters is larger than that used by adults. Some have letter characters that resemble cursive script so that work produced with the program is only a little different from that produced with a pen. This style of type is popular with children who do not want to appear 'different' from children who use a pen to record on paper. Programs with these specific facilities are often available via local education authorities and also with many normal word-processing programs.

Auxiliary programmes which are used with the chosen word-processing program are also available. The word-processing program is loaded, followed by the auxiliary program, which is displayed at the bottom of the screen. The auxiliary program can be used to display vocabulary, ideas or information needed for a specific piece of work, or work that is new to the child. Any of the words displayed can be inserted into the text of the word-processing program by means of the mouse or trackerball (Figure 4.11). Such programs are useful for teachers, who are enabled to provide supporting material very quickly for a child using a word processor.

Children who use word proccessing will often find that other programs which facilitate practice with mathematical concepts, spelling, drawing diagrams, charts and graphs areuseful. These are areas in which those who have difficulty with handwriting will also have difficulty. Some of these types of program are available as part of computer packages. Others are available from companies that supply educational packages. Some of these companies are listed in the 'Useful addresses' section at the end of the text.

Figure 4.11 An ergonomic keyboard with a trackball in a central position which allows it to be used by either forefinger or thumb. The trackball is used instead of a mouse. It has the advantage of being activated without the user removing the hands from the keyboard. It would be useful for children who use supplementary programmes such as Clicker which are usually activated by the mouse.

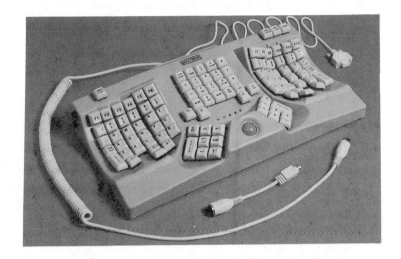

CHAPTER 5

Methods of teaching keyboarding skills

Before beginning to teach any child keyboarding skills it is essential that the person helping the child has the following skills and knowledge:

- familiarity with the equipment that will be used.
- familiarity with the word-processing or other type of program that will be used
- a fair degree of keyboarding skills
- knowledge of the symptoms of the child's disability which are relevant to learning word-processing skills.

Confidence and familiarity with the equipment being used

Knowledge of the equipment to be used is vital so that full attention may be given to the child who is being taught keyboarding skills. Time should be spent with the equipment, learning its functions. This can be done either by studying the appropriate manual or working with someone who is familiar with the equipment and who can teach the necessary skills. When learning keyboarding skills nothing is as important as practical experience. This knowledge is important for the teacher's confidence as well as to inspire confidence in the pupil.

Familiarity with the word-processing program

For similar reasons, the teacher should be familiar with the word-processing program that will be used. Today many programs have similar elements, though details will, of course, differ. The best way to learn about the functions of a program is by practical experience – actually using the program and all its functions. This is far superior to simply studying a manual about it. Reading about the facilities of a particular program will not highlight its idiosyncrasies. Nor will it define those details which may be a problem when it is used with a particular child.

Word-processing skills

Perhaps the most important attribute of people helping children to acquire keyboarding skills is that they themselves have a degree of word-processing skill. This is not to suggest that it is necessary to possess skills at the level of a professional word processer. However there is a need for the following.

- To be conversant with the keyboard and the positions of all the letter characters and other symbols which will be used, to the extent that it is possible to prompt the learner immediately.
- To be conversant with the hand and the digit of that hand which is normally used to fire the different keys. This will allow the teacher to prompt the learner with the finger to be used to fire a particular key as well as to suggest the area of the keyboard where a specific key is located. It is also helpful where fingering needs to be adjusted to suit individual needs.
- To be conversant with the correct method of producing upper case letters and other symbols which require the use of the shift key.
- To have adequate knowledge of layout of the page.
- To appreciate that the acquisition of keyboarding skills requires much practice, concentration and effort.

- To appreciate that there is often a long learning period between having learned the keyboard and being able to use word processing as a useful tool for recording on paper.
- To appreciate that it is a considerable step to progress from copying words to being able to create an original piece of work using word processing. When locating keys and strings of keys becomes completely automatic and takes place without conscious effort, word processing will become a useful means of recording on paper in the classroom.

Knowledge of the child

Children with disabilities usually begin to learn keyboarding skills because they need an efficient and relatively effortless method of recording information, knowledge and ideas. Some of these children will use a word processor for most of their recording for educational purposes, the exceptions being very short pieces of work with words and numbers. For others it will be their only possible means of recording. Some will use word processing for lengthy pieces of work only. A word processor may be necessary for a limited period only, for example during the acute phase of juvenile chronic arthritis or until motor and/or motor planning skills are sufficiently mature to allow the development of swift and legible handwriting.

The person teaching these skills to the child should be aware of any symptoms that require special consideration:

- symptoms that necessitate special seating arrangements
- difficulties with maintaining a stable position
- disabilities associated with impaired hand function, which may include neurological, anatomical, articular difficulties or lack of power
- educational problems associated with the written word
- behavioural problems, such as difficulty with concentration, distractibility and motivation.

Just as there are a number of reasons why some children benefit from learning keyboarding skills, so there are a number of methods of teaching these skills. No single method will suit every child. The aim is not to train children for future secretarial posts or to attain record-breaking speeds in terms of words per minute produced, but to provide children with their personal most efficient means of recording. The levels of efficiency attained will vary greatly between individual children. It may be that one of the teaching methods in this book is suitable exactly as it is presented. Other children may require minor adjustments to a teaching method. Some will need an individualized programme tailored to their specific needs.

Clearly the level of hand function will be an important factor in considering how to teach keyboarding skills. Other factors should also be taken into account, such as educational needs, the philosophy of the school attended, personality and motivation.

Physical needs

There are a large number of conditions which result in handwriting being an unacceptable and impractical method of recording information, knowledge and creative work. These symptoms usually result in the standard methods of acquiring keyboarding skills also being unsuitable. Such children will require carefully adapted methods of learning keyboarding skills. The answers to the following questions will help in making the decision as to whether the acquisition of keyboarding skills is a realistic aim and, if so, exactly how keyboarding skills should be taught.

- Will special seating and/or positioning be required?
- Will word processing be less stressful and less tiring than handwriting?
- Will recording by means of a word processor be quicker than writing by hand?
- Will the simple, repetitive finger movements of word processing leave the child free to concentrate on the content of work?

- Will rapid word processing ever be a realistic aim?
- Is the child able to use only one hand?
- Are some digits completely or partially absent?
- Is there some unsteadiness or tremor in the hands?
- Do the hands lack power?
- Are there problems with visual acuity?
- Are all visual fields intact?
- Are there visual perceptual difficulties, such as problems with figure/background discrimination, position in space or spatial relationships?
- Is there any difficulty with visual accommodation?
- Is there diplopia, nystagmus or other visual problem?
- Is the child enthusiastic about learning keyboarding skills?

Educational needs

Keyboarding skills can be of help to children of various ages and at a variety of educational levels. With some children it will be clear that keyboarding skills will be an advantage and, in some instances, a necessity from an early age. Other children may manage handwritten work in the early years of education when only small amounts are required.

- Keyboarding skills will clearly help those who are following an academic course, or are likely to do so in the future.
- Being able to produce legible notes and work for revision as well as course work and assignments is invaluable.
- Clear, printed notes are easy to work from, especially when revising for exams. This is particularly important if a student's handwriting is difficult to read and there are organizational difficulties with the layout of handwritten work.
- Work produced by word processing is infinitely editable until the desired

layout is obtained. Errors of spelling, sentence construction and overall sequence can be adjusted with ease and, unlike handwritten work, be removed without trace.

- Those who are less academic or perhaps of only limited lexical ability can nonetheless have their educational careers enhanced by the acquisition of keyboarding skills.
- For children who need to put much effort into the production of letter characters and/or have difficulty with motor planning, the use of a word processor will allow them to give most of their attention to the content of their work.
- Even if comparatively little work is produced, its quality and presentation will be greatly enhanced.
- Difficulties with spelling are often reduced because the same words always look exactly the same on the VDU so that words which always present exactly the same pattern will be easier to memorize. Unlike handwritten words, the characters are always consistent and appear in a uniform pattern.
- Learning is also enhanced because not only are the senses of hearing and vision used, but also kinaesthesia, which in this case involves patterns of movement of the fingers over the keys.

Case study

Laura is a woman whose life has been greatly enhanced by her word-processing skills. As a pre-school child she was referred for occupational therapy by her consultant paediatrician. She was diagnosed as having moderate learning difficulties which were, for a number of years, undiagnosed and perhaps hidden by of her excellent reading ability. She had motor learning difficulties at both a gross and fine level in addition to visual perceptual difficulties. She was very much aware of her difficulties, embarrassed by them and often reluctant to attempt activities at which she felt she could not succeed.

Handwriting contains an element of all the skills which Laura found so difficult. Word processing removes the need to produce letter characters by hand and thus the need to describe with a pen or pencil the necessary complex and different letter shapes within the small boundaries of the line of writing. For Laura it was liberation! She learned the keyboard very quickly and was able to record her own sentences. She was a keen cook and enjoyed copying out recipes. None of this was possible with handwriting. Not only had she mastered a new skill but she also grew in self-confidence and self-esteem. Her recording on paper was neat, legible and acceptable to her peers and herself.

She left school at 18 years and undertook a residential course concentrating on independence skills. Laura is now in her mid-twenties and is well able to compose a coherent letter of 300 or 400 words – using a word processor of course.

Personality and motivation

Each child is unique and has individual desires and aspirations, and a level of self-esteem and self-confidence. The importance of conforming with the peer group also varies. Some feel that it is imperative to complete all tasks in exactly the same manner as their peers, while others are happy to use alternative means, in this case word processing to record on paper. These characteristics will affect how the learning of keyboarding skills is approached and the teaching methods used.

Case study

Emma suffers from cerebral palsy of the hemiplegic type. She is a hard-working and very conscientious person. Although she is able to write neatly using her unaffected hand she does adopt a rather tense pen grip. As she writes there is associated movement in her hand on the hemiplegic side; these associated movements together with contractions and spasms cause discomfort and distress. The more prolonged the period of handwriting the more severe these symptoms become and the affected hand becomes very painful.

When Emma was studying for GCSEs she felt very strongly that using a word processor for completing her examination papers would give her an unfair advantage because she was able to produce words with a word processor more quickly than most people are able to write with a pen. She felt that her peers would comment unfavourably about her advantage. Furthermore she felt that having an extra time allowance would be unfair. So Emma completed her examination papers with neither an extra time allowance nor a word processor. Despite her difficulties she was successful in these examinations.

With A levels approaching, her attitude gradually changed and she was happy to have permission to use a word processor to complete her examination papers. Her last contact with her occupational therapist was to request a statement of need to use a word processor at university where she is studying law.

Other children show none of Emma's reluctance and are resolved from the outset that word processing will be their best method of recording on paper. Often, removing the stress and effort of using a pen for prolonged periods allows concentration on the content of work which was not possible when a large amount of concentration and effort was required to use a pen. As in the case study below, a child's perception of education can be radically changed for the better once efficient keyboarding skills are established.

Case study

Peter is an 8-year-old boy who tends to be reticent both at home and more particularly in school. He was referred for occupational therapy because of his handwriting difficulties. Assessment suggested that he had not only difficulties with handwriting but also with other fine and gross motor skills. His handwriting was painfully slow and required his total concentration so that the content of the very small amount of written work was stilted and his sentence construction was very basic. Peter volunteered little spontaneous conversation, tending to answer questions in monosyllables. His eye contact and gestural communication was minimal.

Peter's father and brother were already experts in computing and Peter himself already had a fair amount of knowledge. He was enthusiastic about learning keyboarding skills and had no qualms about being the only user of a laptop computer in his class, indeed in the whole of his primary school. He was loaned a small laptop computer by the local education authority.

He had no difficulty learning the functions of what was an unfamiliar machine and within the first week had studied and assimilated the instruction book! He was well motivated to learn keyboarding skills using the vertical method. Within a month he had mastered the fingering, was conversant with the positions of all the keys and had learned to produce capital letters efficiently. Much more quickly than most children, he was ready to use the laptop for his school work. It was if he was born to use a word processor!

Not only had Peter acquired an effective, stress-free method of recording on paper, he was now able to give his full attention to the content of his work with pleasing results. His output of work recorded on paper greatly increased but continued to be of a very concrete nature. He has no ability for creative writing. He has gained hugely in self-confidence and has more spontaneous conversation, volunteering information quite frequently. Though it may be coincidental, his eye contact has improved and he smiles more frequently. It is now a year since he began to use his laptop in school and, as so often happens, there has been a spontaneous improvement in his handwriting.

School and its philosophies

At secondary school level many teachers prefer projects and assignments to be presented using a word processor. Opinions vary about the use of PCs and laptops for use as a recording tool in the classroom. There are of course some children for whom this is the only option because it is impossible for them to use a pen, or their handwriting is slow and laboured. Philosophies are changing and more schools are accepting word processors as legitimate means of recording on paper.

Sometimes at primary school level the use of word processors is not welcomed. There may be a philosophy that children should be given ample time to acquire handwriting skills. The problem with this attitude is that while the child with problems is labouring to acquire handwriting skills their peers have become proficient. For most children the mechanics of handwriting have been accomplished, so that effort and concentration may be devoted to the content of written work. Children who have problems acquiring handwriting skills are not free to consider the content of their work. They do not gain the same amount of experience as their peers with visual feedback of words which appear in a clear and legible manner on the page. Because they produce only a comparatively small amount of work they do not have practice in using their vocabulary, constructing sentences and the overall planning of a piece of work.

A specific benefit of learning word-processing skills when there are problems with handwriting is that when the two methods of recording on paper are used, there is frequently a spontaneous improvement in handwriting skills. This is thought to be because the imperativeness is removed from the need to become efficient with handwriting when an alternative method of recording on paper is made available. The child develops a more relaxed attitude towards learning handwriting skills and pleasing progress is often made. With some children where there has been initial reluctance on the part of the school to introduce word processing, teachers have, after a time, been known to remark that the child in question's handwriting is now up to standard and really there was no need to learn word processing. This , of course, is untrue, for had the child not had the benefit of word processing – a second and alternative means of recording on paper – the handwriting would not have improved to this extent.

Children and word processors

There is sometimes a belief that when word processing is recommended all that is necessary is to provide the child with a suitable machine, which will henceforth be used effectively by that child in the classroom. This of course is far from the truth; just as a pen is of use only after learning handwriting skills, so it is with word processing. Before children are able to benefit from having a word processor in the classroom they must have a knowledge of keyboarding skills and of the functions of the particular machine being used This cannot be stressed too strongly; there have been occasions when the introduction of a word processor has been disastrous because adequate skills have not been acquired before attempting to use the machine in a practical situation.

Teaching methods

There are two basic methods of teaching keyboarding skills, the vertical and the horizontal. When learning keyboarding skills for commercial purposes the horizontal method is most usually employed. In this method all the fingers and the thumbs are used from the outset. The fingers are placed on the 'home' keys, the positions of other keys being learned relative to the position of the home keys. This method is ideal for people who have no physical, perceptual or specific learning difficulties, but it is not suitable for those who have any of these types of problem.

The second method of learning keyboarding skills is the vertical method, in which the same home keys (see Worksheet 1) are used but specific fingering is learned by each finger in turn. This makes the vertical method, or adaptations of it, suitable for children who are not able to use all their fingers, have absence of some fingers or one hand, or have difficulty with finger gnosis, proprioception or allied difficulties. The method is easily adapted to the number of fingers the child is comfortably able to use. The exercises themselves can be further simplified for children who have memory or sequencing difficulties. For example, the left hand index finger exercise, 'frfvf (space)', may be simplified into two exercises, 'frf (space)' and 'fvf (space)'.

Occasionally, conventional methods of learning the keyboard are not suitable and other systems must be devised. There are, for example, recognized methods of teaching the keyboard for one-handed typists (Richardson 1959). Often an adult hand is able to span the keyboard, but this is not so with children, which makes conventional systems unsuitable. The child with a small hand who is a one-handed word processer will need to move his or her whole hand to be able to use the entire keyboard, resulting in different fingers being used for a particular key depending on the sequence of letters needed to make up a word.

There are some children who may be able to use perhaps only one finger of each hand and have neurological difficulties which will prevent speed being accomplished even after prolonged practice. For such children, conventional methods of acquiring keyboarding skills may not be appropriate. Optimum skills may be best acquired by incorporating keyboarding skills into their progress-to-literacy programme. For those who are already advanced readers and spellers, methods which use frequently used words or letter character strings may be most effective and most rewarding for the child. Indeed, once the keyboard has been learned, these strategies are useful with many children who have the use of all their fingers.

Here are some basic suggestions for teaching keyboarding skills.

- Ensure that the child is sitting in a good position so that there is no physical strain. Support should be provided if necessary. The child should be in a comfortable position so that full attention may be given to developing keyboarding skills without the distraction of discomfort or the conscious effort of maintaining trunk balance.

- Ensure that the working area is well lit by either natural or artificial light. When equipment is battery-operated it can easily be positioned in a good light. This can be more difficult when mains electricity is used and the equipment must be plugged into an accessible electric socket. A reading lamp can solve difficulties of poor lighting when the computer remains in the same position. This is not a practical solution, however, when the equipment is used in a number of situations.

- Have the program ready loaded before the child begins lessons in the early stages. As the child progresses, learning how to load the program and use the menu facilities will become a part of lessons.

- Set up the word processor to produce double line spaces. There is usually an item on the formatting menu which will allow adjustment of line spacing. Double line spacing leaves space between each line of text, which not only makes it easier to read but also sets out the text in approximately the same proportions as handwritten work. Thus the child will be able to compare the amount of work they have produced with that of peers.

- Set the word processor with wide margins on the left- and right-hand sides of the pages. Set margins so that there are approximately 40 characters and spaces per line. This will ensure that the exercises look neat and pleasing on the page. It is very satisfying for a child to see a fresh line of text beginning at quite frequent intervals. It also ensures that those children who have visual scanning, visual saccadic movement or figure/background difficulties are not deterred by overlong lines of text. It also helps those who have problems with the eye movements necessary to flick from the end of one line to the beginning of the next.

- Use the size of letter character most suitable to the child's level of literacy as well as level of visual acuity. For example a 6-year-old would read a book with large print, usually with only a few short lines to a page. Similarly, the handwriting of a 6-year-old child is usually larger and with larger spaces between letters than that of a 10-year-old. A child who has reduced visual acuity will usually have all material in school presented in larger print than do other members of the class.

- Do not use right margin justification or proportional letter character spacing. Both of these facilities alter the regularity of the spacing of the print and are not visually helpful. It is said that print with right justification is more difficult to read.

- Explain to the child how the fingers hover above the home keys. Even if the child is unlikely to use all his or her fingers and thumbs it is usually best to aim for this finger position (see Worksheet 1). Children who use one hand should begin with their fingers hovering over the appropriate home keys (see Worksheets 42 and 73). For a few children this initial position with fingers above the home keys will not be possible or even desirable. Sometimes it will be possible to devise home positions specific to a child's individual needs.

- Either the left or right thumb should fire the space bar, whichever is most convenient at the end of any particular word or group of letter characters. With the fingers hovering over the keys, the thumbs should be in position to fire the space bar. There are exceptions to every rule and one such exception would be the child with hemiplegia who is using only the unimpaired hand to fire the keys. In some instances the hand on the hemiplegic side may be used to fire the space bar. It is worth experimenting to see if this is possible, though if using this hand to fire the space bar is slowing down the speed of work it will be best to work entirely with one hand.

- Should a child be using only one hand on the keyboard it is important to ensure that a symmetrical sitting position is maintained. Children with hemiplegia are apt to sit with the arm they are using for word processing nearer to the table. To prevent this asymmetry, the child's sitting position should be monitored frequently.

- Choose the keyboarding exercises most suitable for the child's abilities. Children who have difficulty with short-term memory or sequencing will cope better with the very simple exercises which contain only a three-key sequence. Each set of exercises is followed by a simplified version which involves only three-key sequences. (All the first exercises of a series for each hand contain only a three-key sequence.)

- *All the worksheets may be photocopied freely.* If the photocopier has suitable facilities, the sheets may be enlarged or reduced to suit the needs of particular children.

- It may be helpful to colour-code the worksheets by photocopying the sheets for the left hand on a different coloured paper from those for the right hand. Ensure that the colours of the paper chosen are sufficiently distinct from each other for the child to appreciate the difference.

- Another method of colour-coding is to place a square of a different bold colour in the top corner of work sheets for the left and right hands. Similar colours could be attached to the left and right sides of the keyboard. Some children are helped by having small stickers of the same colours stuck to back of their right and left hands. Alternatively very small stickers could be attached to each key. (For all colour-coding, I use red for the left (port) side and green for right (starboard) side.) Do ensure that the child has no difficulty with colour discrimination. Consult the child's orthoptist or ophthalmologist about which colours the child can best discriminate between.

- *Each letter character should be named as that key is fired.* This is of great importance, because if the fingers simply fire the keys without heed to which key is being fired the keyboard will not be learned. At first it may be best to say the letters with the child as the keys are fired. This will be essential if the child has poor expressive language skills. It will help to impress on the child how important it is to say the letters as they are fired and will also help to establish a rhythm to the firing of the keys. Whether the name of the letter or the sound of it is said will depend on the level of literacy the child has attained. Older children may prefer to mouth the letters silently.

- The child should also say the word 'space' at the end of each group of letter characters being fired. It is so easy to omit spaces and this practice of saying and thinking about the space where required builds good habits and saves much frustration in the days to come. For example, while working on the first exercise for the right hand the child should say: j - h - j - 'space' - j - h - j - 'space'. This practice will set the child in good stead for producing words so that he or she should not only say or think the letters of each word as the keys are fired, but should also say space at the end of each word, e.g. jug - j - u - g - (space), bun - b - u - n - (space).

- For children who arc using two hands it is important to ensure that the hands hover just above the home keys. Children using only one hand should maintain that hand hovering over its home keys. Initially many children tend to move the hand away from the keyboard immediately a key has been fired. They should be encouraged to maintain a hand position over the home keys.

- Frequent, short practice sessions are best. Five minutes concentrated practice every day is better than half an hour's practice once a week. For some younger children it may be best to have even shorter practice sessions, say two or three minutes. It can be helpful to time the sessions and always finish when that time has elapsed. If the child is doing well it can be tempting to prolong practice. Psychologically it is best to finish a short practice when the child is happy and motivation is high, which will usually lead to a child enthusiastic to begin the next session with a high level of motivation. The child will also be aware that sessions are short, happy occasions.

- Because short practice sessions are usually most effective, it is often better for someone within the school to teach the child keyboarding skills. In some areas it is the practice to involve peripatetic teachers for this purpose. Because these teachers need to travel, perhaps a considerable distance, to see a particular child it would be wasteful to provide only a few minutes' instruction, yet long sessions are counterproductive for many children. A knowledgeable teacher from within the school who provides frequent, brief learning sessions is infinitely preferable.

- Introduce words as soon as possible. This adds to motivation because exercises will be more meaningful than the sequences of letters used for keyboarding exercises. It also introduces the child, where possible, to using both hands together. This helps with body symmetry and gives the child a feel for 'real word processing'! When the keys usually fired by the index fingers have been learned, it is possible to make quite a few words (see Worksheets 36-38). As the keys usually fired by successive fingers are learned, a larger variety of words may be attempted (see Worksheets 39-41).

- When the whole keyboard has been learned, it is a good idea to practise using frequently used words and letter strings (see Worksheets 111-114). These exercises will not only help progress with keyboarding skills but will also help children who have difficulty with learning the spelling of words. In addition to visual and auditory input, the child will learn the keyboard movements necessary to produce these words and thus also have kinaesthetic input. Letter strings such as 'ing', 'str' and 'ent' can be practised so that strings can be used to build words and the positions of these learned on the keyboard. How these ideas are used will depend on the school syllabus and the educational level of the child.

- Learning how to produce upper case or capital letters is a skill which all children need to learn. Many children use the 'caps lock' key to produce capital letters; this should be discouraged for every child except those who have very limited hand function. The usual, most effective and economical method of producing capital letters is by using the shift key. The process is as follows, the shift key is depressed by the fourth finger of the hand not firing the desired letter character or other symbol. The shift key is depressed while the desired key is fired with the other hand. The sequence is: depress the shift key, fire the desired key, release the shift key. Ideally the fourth or little finger should be used on the shift key, though this will not be possible for some children who have or can use only a limited number of fingers for word processing. If it is not possible to use the fourth finger of the hand not firing the desired key to depress the shift key, another finger of that hand should be used. Practice will be required to develop this sequence and use it efficiently. Words requiring capital letters which are appropriate for a particular child should be practised. For example, the child's own name, names of other members of the family, the child's home address, names of nearby towns, countries and other geographical features, the days of the week and the months of the year (see Worksheets 109 and 110).

- Those who have the use of only one hand will need other strategies for producing capital letters. Some with a very small hand will have to resort to the use of the 'caps lock' key. The sequence will be: 'caps lock' on, fire required key, 'caps lock' off. Children will need to practise this sequence, and the exercises suggested for two-handed users will be appropriate. Those with a larger hand will be able to use the shift key on the same side as the required key using a similar method to the two-handed word processer. The finger used to depress the shift key will be either the index/first finger or the little/fourth finger depending on which hand and which side of the keyboard are being used. For example, a child using only the left hand would use the little finger to depress the shift key when firing any letter on the left side of the keyboard up to 't-g-b-'. The same child would use the index finger to depress the shift key when firing any key between 'y-h-n-' and ';p-;-.'.

- Having become conversant with the positions of the letter characters on the keyboard to the extent that the fingers can fire a particular key without searching, it is time to move on to phrases and short sentences. The words these phrases and sentences contain will depend on the educational level of the child as well as any particular interests the child may have. These strings of words should each be repeated a number of times until an even rhythm is established (see Worksheets 115-117).

- As with all practice, the child should be advised to begin slowly, after which speed will, to some degree, ensue. Many children feel that they must fire keys as quickly as possible even in the early stages of learning keyboarding skills. This results in erratic speeds and frustration because of the great number of errors and the inability to maintain the initial speed. Encourage slow, regular firing of keys and, where possible, speed will develop through increasing efficiency and skill.

- Practising keyboarding skills can be tedious and this is one of the reasons why frequent very short periods of practice are advocated. Teaching in stages small enough to ensure success is another way of maintaining motivation.

- Throughout the learning period it should be borne in mind that the aim is not to produce commercial secretaries and word processors but to provide children with their own most efficient and effective means of recording on paper. Except for children who have severe visual problems of a degenerative nature, there is no special virtue in perfect touch-typing.

- Many children learn keyboarding skills, become proficient with various exercises, and are able to copy hand-written and printed material. It may take a further period of time to reach the stage where thoughts can be easily transformed into the printed word. As with children who write by hand, who at first give most of their attention to the mechanics of handwriting with handwriting only later becoming an unconscious activity and the content of the work becoming the subject of effort and concentration, so it is with word processing. A considerable time passes before it becomes an automatic process leaving the worker free to concentrate on the content of the work. This point should always be borne in mind before encouraging a child to use a word processor for the entire school day.

Notes for worksheets

- Home keys: Worksheet 1 for two-handed users; Worksheet 42 for right-handed users; Worksheet 73 for left-handed users.
- Worksheets 2–13: keyboarding exercises for two-handed users.
- Worksheets 14–35: simplified keyboarding exercises for two-handed users.

- Worksheets 36–41: words for fingering practice.
- Worksheets 42–52: keyboarding exercises for right-handed users.
- Worksheets 53–72: simplified keyboarding exercises for right-handed users.
- Worksheets 73–83: keyboarding exercises for left-handed users.
- Worksheets 84–103: simplified keyboarding exercises for left-handed users.
- Some children will not yet be using all the punctuation marks on keys at the right-hand side of the keyboard. Exercises which contain such keys should be omitted until needed.
- Worksheet 104: words that are often used.
- Worksheets 105 and 106 contain words formed by letter characters which are on adjacent keys. These worksheets are particularly useful when only one hand may be used.
- Worksheets 107 and 108 contain words with letter characters at opposite ends of the keyboard.
- Worksheets 109 and 110 provide practice with producing capital letters.
- Worksheets 111–113 contain frequently used letter strings.
- Worksheet 114 contains sound blends.
- Worksheets 115–117 contain sentences to copy and complete.
- Worksheets 118–120 contain outlines of hands on the fingers of which the letters to be fired by each one may be marked. Worksheet 118 is for two-handed users, 119 for right hand only and 120 for the left hand only. Thus it will be possible to provide a precise fingering plan to suit the needs of all children.
- Worksheets that will be used by a number of children will be more durable if they are photocopied, colour-coded and then laminated.

References

Attwood T (1998) Asperger's Syndrome: a guide for parents and professionals. London: Jessica Kingsley Publishers.

Craft AW (1985) Arthritis in children. Paediatric symposium. British Journal of Hospital Medicine 33(4): 188–94.

Downey JA, Low NL (1982) The Child with Disabling Illness. Principles of rehabilitation. New York: Raven Press.

Fahn S (1972) Differential diagnosis of tremors: symposium on clinical neurology. Medical Clinics of North America 6(6): 1363–75.

Griffiths ID, Craft AW (1988) Management of juvenile chronic arthritis. Hospital Update 14(4): 1372–84.

Hosking G (1982) An Introduction to Paediatric Neurology. London: Faber and Faber.

Hulme C, Lord R (1986) Clumsy children – a review of recent research. Child Care, Health and Development 12(4): 257–69.

Illingworth R (1983) The Development of the Infant and Young Child. Edinburgh: Churchill Livingstone.

Johnson W, Schwartz G, Barbeau, A (1962) Studies in dystonia musculorum deformans. Archives of Neurology 7: 301–13.

Jones K (1988) Smith's Recognisable Patterns of Human Malformation. Philadelphia, London, Toronto: WB Saunders.

Nolan C (1981) Damburst of Dreams. London: Pan Books.

Nolan C (1987) Under the Eye of the Clock. London: Weidenfeld and Nicholson.

Penso DE (1992) The mucopolysaccharidoses: classification, symptoms and the role of the occupational therapist. British Journal of Occupational Therapy 55(2): 44–8.

Richardson NK (1959) Type with One Hand. USA: South Western Publishing.

Sheridan M (1975) From Birth to Five Years. London: NFER-Nelson.

Springer SP, Deutsch G (1989) Left Brain, Right Brain. New York: WH Freeman and Company.

Stansfield J (1997) A First Handbook of IT and Special Educational Needs. Tamworth, Staffs: NASEN Enterprises.

Warnock M (1978) Special Educational Needs: report of the Committee of Enquiry into Education of Handicapped Children and Young People. London: HMSO.

Further reading

Anderson E (1976) Impairment of motor (manual skill) in children with spina bifida, myelomeningocele and hydrocephalus. British Journal of Occupational Therapy 39(4): 91–3.

Ansell B (1981) When Your Child has Arthritis. Arthritis and Rheumatism Council for Research, 41 Eagle Street, London WC1R 4AR.

Beran R (1982) Learning About Epilepsy. Medical Information Services Ltd, 36/37 Pembroke Street, Oxford OX1 1BL.

Briggs D (1980) A study of the influence of handwriting upon grades using examination scripts. Educational Review 32(2): 185–93.

Brown B, Henderson S (1989) A sloping desk? Should the wheel turn full circle? Handwriting Review 3: 55–9.

Day J (Ed) (1995) Access Technology Making the Right Choice. Coventry: National Council for Educational Technology.

Finnie N (1974) Handling the Young Cerebral Palsied Child at Home. London: William Heinemann Medical Books.

Gailey P (1997) Using word processing to assist writing for students with learning disabilities. School System: Special Interest Quarterly 4(4). USA: American Occupational Therapy Association, Inc., 4720 Montgomery Lane, Bethesda, MD 20814-3425.

Handley J (1986) Posture education in primary schools. Health at School 1(6): 176–7; 1(7): 220–1; 1(8): 259–60.

Hartveld A (1998) Key decisions. Remedial Therapist 24(27): 5.

Haskell H, Barrett K (1989) The Education of Children with Motor and Neurological Disabilities. London: Chapman & Hall; New York: Nichols Publishing.

Hawkins S, Gadsby M (1991) Perceptuo-motor deficit: a major learning difficulty. British Journal of Occupational Therapy 54(4): 145–9.

Hoare D, Larking D (1991) Kinaesthetic abilities of clumsy children. Developmental and Child Neurology 33(6): 671–8.

Kashani J (1986) Self-esteem of handicapped children and adolescents. Developmental Medicine and Child Neurology 28(1): 77–83

King-Thomas L, Hacker B (Eds) (1987) A Therapist's Guide to Paediatric Assessment. Boston/Toronto: Little Brown and Company.

Lee M, French J (undated) Dyspraxia – a handbook for therapists. London: Association of Paediatric Chartered Physiotherapists.

Losse H, Henderson S et al (1991) Clumsiness in children – do they grow out of it? Developmental Medicine and Child Neurology 33(1): 55–68.

McKinlay I (1987) Children with motor learning difficulties: not so much a syndrome – more a way of life. Physiotherapy 73(11): 653–8.

Miller E, Setlis L (1971) The effects of hydrocephalus on perception. Developmental Medicine and Child Neurology 13: 77.

Myers P (1987) The sloping board. Handwriting Review 1: 43.

Penso D (1987) Occupational Therapy for Children with Disabilities. London: Croom Helm.

Penso D (1987) The key to legibility. Therapy Weekly 14(23): 4.

Penso D (1990) Keyboard, Graphic and Handwriting Skills: helping people with motor disabilities. London: Chapman & Hall.

Penso D (1992) Perceptuo-motor Difficulties: theory and strategies to help children, adolescents and adults. London: Chapman & Hall.

Poustie J (1997) Solutions for Specific Learning Difficulties. Somerset: Next Generation.

Restricted Growth Association (1989) The Layman's Guide to Restricted Growth. 103 St Thomas Avenue, Hayling Island, Hampshire PO11 0EU.

Tyerman A (undated) Psychological effects of head injury. Headway, The National Head Injuries Association, 7 King Edward Court, King Edward Street, Nottingham NG1 1EW.

Glossary

Accommodation, visual The process by which the eye focuses on to an object. This is brought about by the movement of the eye muscles which adjust the curvature and thickness of the lens.

Amblyopia A condition characterized by low visual acuity without any apparent lesion of the eye or proven disorder of the visual pathways and which is not correctable by optical means.

Amnion:(*adjective* amniotic) The innermost membrane enveloping the fetus (the child in the uterus).

Associated movements Unintended movements that accompany an intended movement. For example, a child's early attempts at writing with a pencil may be accompanied by tongue movements which roughly mirror the movements of the hand.

Athetosis Involuntary writhing movements due to cerebral malfunction. A symptom of one type of cerebral palsy.

Atlanto-axial joint The joint between the first two vertebrae (bones) of the spinal column (the backbone). The first vertebra, the atlas, supports the globe of the head. The second vertebra, the axis, provides the pivot upon which the atlas and, with it, the skull rotate.

Autosomal recessive A type of genetic inheritance pattern in which an individual carrying the affected gene will not be affected by it. Should a man and a woman who both carry this affected gene produce children there will be a 25% chance of the child of each pregnancy being affected.

Binocular vision When both eyes contribute towards producing a percept.

Cerebellum (*adjective* cerebellar) The part of the brain at the back of the head which lies beneath the cerebrum (the large part of the brain occupying most of the skull) and above the medulla oblongata (the part of the spinal cord which lies within the skull). The cerebellum co-ordinates impulses from the organs of balance and from the joints. It monitors impulses coming from the brain to ensure that the movement follows the intended path. It maintains the normal tone of the muscles by its action on the brainstem. Damage to the cerebellum results in an unsteady gait, incoordination and hypotonia (low muscle tone).

Cerebral cortex The external layer of the cerebrum, the largest area of the brain which is divided into the right and left hemispheres.

Cerebrospinal fluid The clear fluid that bathes the brain and spinal cord.

Cerebrovascular accident (CVA) Temporary or permanent damage to part of the brain caused by haemorrhage, a blood clot in a cerebral blood vessel or physical damage to part of the brain. The effects of the damage will depend on the area of the brain involved, the effect being manifested on the opposite side of the body to the site of the damage. Vision and language may also be involved. Other names for CVA include stroke and seizure.

Congenital Present at birth.

Connective tissue Tissue that supports and connects organs and structures of the body. The term is often used to describe the tissue around joints.

Contracture Permanent contraction of a part of the body, most usually occurring in the upper or lower limb, which is caused by the formation of inelastic fibrous tissue.

Cranial Of the skull or cranium.

Distal Situated furthest from the centre of the body. For example the final joints of the fingers are the distal joints.

Dorsi-flexion The movement of elevating the foot so that the angle at the ankle joint between the foot and the leg is reduced.

Dycem A non-slip material which is available either on a roll, which can be cut to the required size and shape, or in the form of ready-made mats of various sizes. Dycem may be used to prevent all manner of objects from slipping including paper, books, computers, dishes and plates.

Dyspraxia Difficulty with planning and organizing movements at a cerebral level. Dyspraxia can affect any or all executive skills from self-help activities to handwriting and speech.

Epiphysis The end of a long bone developed separately but attached by cartilage to the shaft of the bone. It is at this junction between the epiphysis and the shaft that growth takes place. When growth is complete the epiphysis unites with the shaft of the bone.

Executive language skills The planning and realization of communication most usually resulting in speech.

Executive skills Motor activities or movements. They may be large movements of the body, fine hand and finger movements or speech.

Extra-pyramidal tracts The constituent fibres of these nerve pathways unconsciously modify the activities of the pyramidal system. The pyramidal system consists of nerves concerned with movement which originate in the brain and form part of the spinal nerve, which is housed within the backbone.

Flexion Bending of a joint.

Gestalt A configuration, pattern or organized whole with qualities different from those of its components separately considered.

High-frequency deafness Deafness which affects the higher sound frequency while lower frequencies are intact. High-frequency deafness occurs quite frequently in athetoid cerebral palsy.

In utero In the uterus. The term usually refers to a child before birth.

Kinaesthesia This is the sensation which results from the tension and position of joints and muscles. It is an additional sensory channel by which learning can takes place. An example of such learning would be tracing the shapeof a letter character with the finger, whose joint positions and tension of muscles would undergo subtle changes during the process.

Kyphosis An abnormal curve of the spinal column in a posterior direction giving a hump-backed appearance. Sometimes the curvature is in both a poster-ior and a lateral direction when it is known as a kypho-scoliosis.

Language skills The entire range of linguistic abilities, including the comprehension of language, the mental formulation of language, executive and articulatory skills.

Lordosis An abnormal forward curve of the spine in the lumbar region (lower back), giving a hollow-backed appearance.

Lumbar Pertaining to the loins.

Motor learning difficulties Problems with learning the skills of movement in the absence of general sensory and intellectual handicaps. A further criter-ion is that there are no hard neurological signs. Other terms which have been used for this condition are clumsy child syndrome, developmental co-ordination disorder and (erroneously) dyspraxia.

Nystagmus A regular, repetitive and involuntary movement of the eye with variable direction, amplitude and frequency. The direction of these abnormal eye movements may be vertical, horizontal, diagonal or rotatory. People with a nystagmus will usually find the fields of vision where the nystagmus is least troublesome and hold their head in such a position that these optimum fields of vision are used.

Occupational therapist A professionally qualified person who treats physical and psychiatric conditions through specific activities in order to help people reach their maximum level of function and independence in all aspects of daily life.

Orthoses Splints used to support, prevent strain, maintain position and correct deformity of body parts.

Orthotist A person skilled in the manufacture of orthoses or splints.

Orthoptist A person who practises orthoptics, which is the study, diagnosis and non-operative treatment of anomalies of binocular vision, strabismus (squint) and monocular functional amblyopia (low visual acuity).

Paramedical Beside or ancillary to the medical. Therapists are sometimes described as paramedical.

Perinatal Around the time of birth, which includes the period before birth, birth, and the period following birth.

Peripheral vision Vision resulting from stimulation of the retina outside the fovea, a condition in which only the outer parts of the retina are stimulated.

Peritoneal Within the membranous lining of the abdominal cavity.

Physiotherapist A person who treats disease, disability or injury by physical means, most usually by active methods requiring the co-operation of the person being treated. It is concerned with the maintenance of posture and active movement.

Refractive disorders (of the eye) Conditions in which there is relaxed accommodation and the image of objects at infinity is not formed on the retina. The result is blurred vision. Conditions in which this type of visual error occurs are astigmatism, hypermetropia and myopia.

Saccadic movements The short rapid movement of the eye which occurs when reading a line of print or when fixating from one point to another. Children who have difficulty with these eye movements may find scanning a page or screen of print difficult.

Sacral Relating to the sacrum, the triangular bone which forms the back of the pelvis.

Scoliosis An abnormal curvature of the spine in a lateral direction. Sometimes the curvature is in both a posterior and a lateral direction, when it is known as a kypho-scoliosis. See also **lordosis**.

Spasm (muscle) A sudden involuntary contraction of one or more muscles. Muscle spasm is a symptom of cerebral palsy, which greatly affects co-ordin-ated movements.

Speech and language therapist A professionally qualified person who treats those who have a language disorder, which may be congenital or acquired. Such disorders include difficulty with comprehension of language, difficulty with expressive language and problems with articulation. Aims may be to facilitate spoken language or to provide an alternative means of communication such as a system of signing.

Symptom A term applied to any evidence of a disease. Strictly it is applied to subjective evidence of the person who is experiencing the symptoms. The term 'sign' is usually applied to symptoms of which the patient does not complain but which are elicited upon physical examination.

Syndrome A group of symptoms or characteristics, all or most of which occur in a particular disorder.

Tendo-calcaneum The unification of the tendons of two muscles in the back of the leg, soleus and gastrocnemius, which is inserted into the calcaneus, the heel bone. This tendon is sometimes known as the Achilles tendon or tendo Achilles.

Thoracic Relating to the thorax.

Tremor An involuntary trembling of voluntary muscles (those used for movement). The amplitude of the tremor may vary from very fine (10-12 vibrations per second) to coarse. The characteristics of tremors are various and include intention tremor where the tremor intensifies when movement is attempted.

Tunnel vision Vision limited to the central part of the visual field as though looking through a hollow cylindrical tube. Tunnel vision limits the area which can be scanned visually. Head movements are used to compensate for the reduced visual fields.

Visual acuity The capacity for seeing distinctly the details of an object.

Visual fields The extent of space in which objects are visible to an eye in a given position. The visual field extends to approximately 100 degrees horizontally outwards, 60 degrees nasally, 65 degrees upwards and 75 degrees downwards when the eye is in a straight forward position.

X-linked This term refers to the chromosomes. Females have two X chromosomes and males one X chromosome and one Y chromosome. Inherited conditions which are carried by genes on the X chromosome are described as X-linked.

Useful addresses

ACE Advisory Centre for Education
1B Aberdeen Studios
22–24 Highbury Grove
London N5 2EA

Arm and Hand Deficiencies
'Reach'
32–33 Victoria Road
Surbiton
Surrey KT6 4JT

Arthrogryposis Group
1 The Oaks
Gillingham
Dorset SP8 4SW

Asperger Syndrome Support Network
National Autistic Society
276 Willesden Lane
London NW2 5RB

ASBAH, Association for Spina Bifida and
Hydrocephalus
42 Park Road
Peterborough
Cambridgeshire PE1 2UQ

Association of Paediatric Chartered
Physiotherapists
c/o Chartered Society of Physiotherapists
14 Bedford Row
London WC1R 4ED

Ataxia Group
Copse Edge
Thursley Road
Elstead
Godalming
Surrey GU8 6DJ

British Association of Occupational
Therapists Ltd
106–114 Borough High Street
London SE1 1LB
The official body for all aspects of occupa-
tional therapy.

British Dyslexia Association Computer
Resource Centre
Department of Psychology
University of Hull
Hull HU6 7RX

The Centre has a range of software which has
been found to be of value for children who
have dyslexia.
British Epilepsy Association
Anstey House
40 Hanover Square
Leeds LS3 1BE

British Orthoptist Society
Tavistock House North
Tavistock Square
London WC1H 9HX

Brittle Bone Society
112 City Road
Dundee DD2 2PW

Children's Chronic Arthritis Association
47 Battenhall Avenue
Worcester WR5 2HN

Computers in Education: Advisory Unit
126 Great North Road
Hatfield
Hertfordshire AL9 5JZ

The unit produces software and offers advice, training and technical support in the use of computers with children who have learning or physical disabilities.

Congenital Muscular Dystrophy Support Group
21 Morrison Drive
Pitcorthie
Dunfermline
Fife KY11 5DJ

Contact a Family
170 Tottenham Court Road
London W1P 0HA

A directory of specific conditions and rare conditions which is revised at frequent intervals.

Crick Software Ltd
1 The Avenue
Spinney Hill
Northampton NN3 6BA

Programs with an on-screen grid that can contain a letter character, word or phrase, which can be inserted into a word-processing program using the mouse.

Disabled Living Foundation
380–384 Harrow Road
London W9 2HU

Provides information on all aspects of disability.
The Dyslexia Association
98 London Road
Reading
Berkshire RG1 5AU

The Dyspraxia Foundation
8 West Alley
Hitchin
Herts SG5 1EG

The foundation supports both children and adults who suffer from their definition of dyspraxia: 'an impairment or immaturity of the organization of movement and, in many individuals, there may be associated problems with language, perception and thought'.

The Dystonia Society
Omnibus Workspace
41 North Road
London N7 9DP

Facio Scapulo Humeral Muscular Dystrophy Support Group
2 Hamlyn Close
Pipers Green Lane
Edgware
Middlcscx HA8 8BD

Granada Learning Ltd
SEMERC
1 Broadbent Road
Watersheddings
Oldham OL1 4LB

One of the major suppliers of computer software and training for people with special needs. SEMERC has a variety of special keyboards, including ultra compact, lower-case letters and large keys. They also have keyguards and keyboard skins. There is a network of centres throughout UK which provide training, advice and support.

HEADWAY National Head Injuries Association Ltd
7 King Edward Court
King Edward Street
Nottingham NG1 1EW

Hemi-Help
166 Boundaries Road
London SW12 8HG
Offers support, a quarterly newsletter and workshops for families with a child with hemiplegia.

Hyperactive Children's Support Group
71 Whyke Lane
Chichester
West Sussex PO19 2LD

Jennifer Trust for Spinal Muscular Atrophy
11 Ash Tree Close
Wellesbourne
Warwick CV35 9SA

P.C.D. Maltron Ltd
15 Orchard Lane
East Molesey
Surrey KT8 0BN

Ergonomic keyboards for two- and one-handed users and other specialist equipment.

Muscular Dystrophy Group of Great Britain and Northern Ireland
7–11 Prescott Place
London SW4 6BS

NAPOT, National Association of Paediatric Occupational Therapists
NAPOT is a special interest group of the British Association of Occupational Therapy. Members are specialists who have experience and knowledge in the field of children who have some area of special need. Many members will have specialist knowledge of helping children who have specific difficulty with recording information on paper.

NASEN Enterprises Ltd
NASEN House
4/5 Amber Business Village
Amber Close
Amington
Tamworth
Staffs B77 4RP

NASEN, National Association of Special Educational Needs, is an organization that represents professionals working in the area of special educational needs. It runs conferences and seminars locally and nationally. NASEN Enterprises Ltd publishes material on aspects of the education of children with special educational needs, including information technology.

NCET, National Council for Educational Technology
Milburn Hill Road
Science Park
Coventry CV4 7JJ

NCET provides information on computers and software. It produces specialist publications related to specific learning difficulties.

National Federation of ACCESS Centres
Hereward College
Bramston Crescent
Tile Hill Lane
Coventry CV4 9SW

A network of centres in further and higher education which provide support, assessment and training for students with disabilities.

Philip and Tacey
North Way
Andover
Hampshire SP10 5BA

Suppliers of portable sloping surfaces suitable for use under a keyboard.

The Raynaud's and Scleroderma Association
112 Crewe Road
Alsager
Cheshire ST7 2JA

Restricted Growth Association
c/o Contact a Family
170 Tottenham Court Road
London W1P 0HA

A self-help group concerned with the well-being of people with restricted growth. There is a medical committee that disseminates specialist advice to other clinicians.

SCOPE (formerly The Spastics Society)
Library and Information Department
12 Park Crescent
London W1N 4EQ

The Society for Mucopolysaccharide Diseases
55 Hill Avenue
Amersham HP6 5BX

Offers information, advice and support. Families can be put in touch with other families who have a child with a similar condition. There is an annual family conference as well as regional meetings.

Worksheets

Worksheet 1

Word processing with two hands

Home keys

Left hand

4th finger	3rd finger	2nd finger	1st finger
a	s	d	f

Always begin with your fingers on these keys

Word processing with two hands

Right hand

1st finger	2nd finger	3rd finger	4th finger
j	k	l	;

Your thumbs will be ready to use the space bar

Worksheet 2

Word processing with two hands

1st finger left hand

f g f (space)

Say the letters and spaces as you work

Make a block of this group of letters like this:

fgf fgf fgf fgf fgf fgf fgf
fgf fgf fgf fgf fgf fgf fgf
fgf fgf fgf fgf fgf fgf fgf
fgf fgf fgf fgf fgf fgf fgf
fgf fgf fgf fgf fgf fgf fgf
fgf fgf fgf fgf fgf fgf fgf

Worksheet 3

Word processing with two hands

1st finger left hand

f r f v f (space)

Say the letters and spaces as you work

Make a block of this group of letters like this:

frfvf frfvf frfvf frfvf frfvf frfvf
frfvf frfvf frfvf frfvf frfvf frfvf
frfvf frfvf frfvf frfvf frfvf frfvf
frfvf frfvf frfvf frfvf frfvf frfvf
frfvf frfvf frfvf frfvf frfvf frfvf
frfvf frfvf frfvf frfvf frfvf frfvf

Word processing with two hands

1st finger left hand

f t f b f (space)

Say the letters and spaces as you work

Make a block of this group of letters like this:

ftfbf ftfbf ftfbf ftfbf ftfbf ftfbf
ftfbf ftfbf ftfbf ftfbf ftfbf ftfbf
ftfbf ftfbf ftfbf ftfbf ftfbf ftfbf
ftfbf ftfbf ftfbf ftfbf ftfbf ftfbf
ftfbf ftfbf ftfbf ftfbf ftfbf ftfbf
ftfbf ftfbf ftfbf ftfbf ftfbf ftfbf

Word processing with two hands

1st finger right hand

j h j (space)

Say the letters and spaces as you work

Make a block of this group of letters like this:

jhj jhj jhj jhj jhj jhj jhj
jhj jhj jhj jhj jhj jhj jhj
jhj jhj jhj jhj jhj jhj jhj
jhj jhj jhj jhj jhj jhj jhj
jhj jhj jhj jhj jhj jhj jhj
jhj jhj jhj jhj jhj jhj jhj

Worksheet 6

Word processing with two hands

1st finger right hand

j u j m j (space)

Say the letters and spaces as you work

Make a block of this group of letters like this:

jujmj jujmj jujmj jujmj jujmj
jujmj jujmj jujmj jujmj jujmj
jujmj jujmj jujmj jujmj jujmj
jujmj jujmj jujmj jujmj jujmj
jujmj jujmj jujmj jujmj jujmj
jujmj jujmj jujmj jujmj jujmj

Word processing with two hands

1st finger right hand

j y j n j (space)

Say the letters and spaces as you work

Make a block of this group of letters like this:

jyjnj jyjnj jyjnj jyjnj jyjnj
jyjnj jyjnj jyjnj jyjnj jyjnj
jyjnj jyjnj jyjnj jyjnj jyjnj
jyjnj jyjnj jyjnj jyjnj jyjnj
jyjnj jyjnj jyjnj jyjnj jyjnj
jyjnj jyjnj jyjnj jyjnj jyjnj

Word processing with two hands

2nd finger left hand

d e d c d (space)

Say the letters and spaces as you work

Make a block of this group of letters like this:

dedcd dedcd dedcd dedcd dedcd
dedcd dedcd dedcd dedcd dedcd
dedcd dedcd dedcd dedcd dedcd
dedcd dedcd dedcd dedcd dedcd
dedcd dedcd dedcd dedcd dedcd
dedcd dedcd dedcd dedcd dedcd

Word processing with two hands

3rd finger left hand

S W S X S (space)

Say the letters and spaces as you work

Make a block of this group of letters like this:

SWSXS SWSXS SWSXS SWSXS SWSXS

SWSXS SWSXS SWSXS SWSXS SWSXS

SWSXS SWSXS SWSXS SWSXS SWSXS

SWSXS SWSXS SWSXS SWSXS SWSXS

SWSXS SWSXS SWSXS SWSXS SWSXS

SWSXS SWSXS SWSXS SWSXS SWSXS

Word processing with two hands

2nd finger right hand

k i k , k (space)

Say the letters and spaces as you work

Make a block of this group of letters like this:

kik,k kik,k kik,k kik,k kik,k
kik,k kik,k kik,k kik,k kik,k
kik,k kik,k kik,k kik,k kik,k
kik,k kik,k kik,k kik,k kik,k
kik,k kik,k kik,k kik,k kik,k
kik,k kik,k kik,k kik,k kik,k

Word processing with two hands

3rd finger right hand

l o l . l (space)

Say the letters and spaces as you work

Make a block of this group of letters like this:

lol.l lol.l lol.l lol.l lol.l
lol.l lol.l lol.l lol.l lol.l
lol.l lol.l lol.l lol.l lol.l
lol.l lol.l lol.l lol.l lol.l
lol.l lol.l lol.l lol.l lol.l
lol.l lol.l lol.l lol.l lol.l

Word processing with two hands

4th finger left hand

a q a z a (space)

Say the letters and spaces as you work

Make a block of this group of letters like this:

aqaza aqaza aqaza aqaza aqaza
aqaza aqaza aqaza aqaza aqaza
aqaza aqaza aqaza aqaza aqaza
aqaza aqaza aqaza aqaza aqaza
aqaza aqaza aqaza aqaza aqaza
aqaza aqaza aqaza aqaza aqaza

Word processing with two hands

4th finger right hand

; p ; / ; (space)

Say the letters and spaces as you work

Make a block of this group of letters like this:

;p;/; ;p;/; ;p;/; ;p;/; ;p;/;
;p;/; ;p;/; ;p;/; ;p;/; ;p;/;
;p;/; ;p;/; ;p;/; ;p;/; ;p;/;
;p;/; ;p;/; ;p;/; ;p;/; ;p;/;
;p;/; ;p;/; ;p;/; ;p;/; ;p;/;
;p;/; ;p;/; ;p;/; ;p;/; ;p;/;

Worksheet 14

Word processing with two hands
Simplified

1st finger left hand

f g f (space)

Say the letters and spaces as you work

Make a block of this group of letters like this:

fgf fgf fgf fgf fgf fgf fgf
fgf fgf fgf fgf fgf fgf fgf
fgf fgf fgf fgf fgf fgf fgf
fgf fgf fgf fgf fgf fgf fgf
fgf fgf fgf fgf fgf fgf fgf
fgf fgf fgf fgf fgf fgf fgf

Word processing with two hands
Simplified

1st finger right hand

j h j   (space)

Say the letters and spaces as you work

Make a block of this group of letters like this:

jhj jhj jhj jhj jhj jhj jhj
jhj jhj jhj jhj jhj jhj jhj
jhj jhj jhj jhj jhj jhj jhj
jhj jhj jhj jhj jhj jhj jhj
jhj jhj jhj jhj jhj jhj jhj
jhj jhj jhj jhj jhj jhj jhj

Word processing with two hands
Simplified

1st finger left hand

f r f (space)

Say the letters and spaces as you work

Make a block of this group of letters like this:

frf frf frf frf frf frf frf
frf frf frf frf frf frf frf
frf frf frf frf frf frf frf
frf frf frf frf frf frf frf
frf frf frf frf frf frf frf
frf frf frf frf frf frf frf

Word processing with two hands
Simplified

1st finger left hand

f v f (space)

Say the letters and spaces as you work

Make a block of this group of letters like this:

fvf fvf fvf fvf fvf fvf
fvf fvf fvf fvf fvf fvf
fvf fvf fvf fvf fvf fvf
fvf fvf fvf fvf fvf fvf
fvf fvf fvf fvf fvf fvf
fvf fvf fvf fvf fvf fvf

Worksheet 18

Word processing with two hands
Simplified

1st finger left hand

f t f (space)

Say the letters and spaces as you work

Make a block of this group of letters like this:

ftf ftf ftf ftf ftf ftf ftf
ftf ftf ftf ftf ftf ftf ftf
ftf ftf ftf ftf ftf ftf ftf
ftf ftf ftf ftf ftf ftf ftf
ftf ftf ftf ftf ftf ftf ftf
ftf ftf ftf ftf ftf ftf ftf

Worksheet 19

Word processing with two hands
Simplified

1st finger left hand

f b f (space)

Say the letters and spaces as you work

Make a block of this group of letters like this:

fbf fbf fbf fbf fbf fbf fbf
fbf fbf fbf fbf fbf fbf fbf
fbf fbf fbf fbf fbf fbf fbf
fbf fbf fbf fbf fbf fbf fbf
fbf fbf fbf fbf fbf fbf fbf
fbf fbf fbf fbf fbf fbf fbf

Word processing with two hands
Simplified

1st finger right hand

j u j (space)

Say the letters and spaces as you work

Make a block of this group of letters like this:

juj juj juj juj juj juj juj
juj juj juj juj juj juj juj
juj juj juj juj juj juj juj
juj juj juj juj juj juj juj
juj juj juj juj juj juj juj
juj juj juj juj juj juj juj

Word processing with two hands
Simplified

1st finger right hand

j m j (space)

Say the letters and spaces as you work

Make a block of this group of letters like this:

jmj jmj jmj jmj jmj jmj jmj
jmj jmj jmj jmj jmj jmj jmj
jmj jmj jmj jmj jmj jmj jmj
jmj jmj jmj jmj jmj jmj jmj
jmj jmj jmj jmj jmj jmj jmj
jmj jmj jmj jmj jmj jmj jmj

Worksheet 22

Word processing with two hands
Simplified

1st finger right hand

j y j (space)

Say the letters and spaces as you work

Make a block of this group of letters like this:

jyj jyj jyj jyj jyj jyj jyj
jyj jyj jyj jyj jyj jyj jyj
jyj jyj jyj jyj jyj jyj jyj
jyj jyj jyj jyj jyj jyj jyj
jyj jyj jyj jyj jyj jyj jyj
jyj jyj jyj jyj jyj jyj jyj

Word processing with two hands
Simplified

1st finger right hand

j n j (space)

Say the letters and spaces as you work

Make a block of this group of letters like this:

jnj jnj jnj jnj jnj jnj jnj
jnj jnj jnj jnj jnj jnj jnj
jnj jnj jnj jnj jnj jnj jnj
jnj jnj jnj jnj jnj jnj jnj
jnj jnj jnj jnj jnj jnj jnj
jnj jnj jnj jnj jnj jnj jnj

Word processing with two hands
Simplified

2nd finger left hand

d e d (space)

Say the letters and spaces as you work

Make a block of this group of letters like this:

ded ded ded ded ded ded ded
ded ded ded ded ded ded ded
ded ded ded ded ded ded ded
ded ded ded ded ded ded ded
ded ded ded ded ded ded ded
ded ded ded ded ded ded ded

Word processing with two hands
Simplified

2nd finger left hand

d c d (space)

Say the letters and spaces as you work

Make a block of this group of letters like this:

dcd dcd dcd dcd dcd dcd dcd
dcd dcd dcd dcd dcd dcd dcd
dcd dcd dcd dcd dcd dcd dcd
dcd dcd dcd dcd dcd dcd dcd
dcd dcd dcd dcd dcd dcd dcd
dcd dcd dcd dcd dcd dcd dcd

Word processing with two hands
Simplified

2nd finger right hand

k i k (space)

Say the letters and spaces as you work

Make a block of this group of letters like this:

kik kik kik kik kik kik kik
kik kik kik kik kik kik kik
kik kik kik kik kik kik kik
kik kik kik kik kik kik kik
kik kik kik kik kik kik kik
kik kik kik kik kik kik kik

Word processing with two hands
Simplified

2nd finger right hand

k , k (space)

Say the letters and spaces as you work

Make a block of this group of letters like this:

k,k k,k k,k k,k k,k k,k k,k
k,k k,k k,k k,k k,k k,k k,k
k,k k,k k,k k,k k,k k,k k,k
k,k k,k k,k k,k k,k k,k k,k
k,k k,k k,k k,k k,k k,k k,k
k,k k,k k,k k,k k,k k,k k,k

Word processing with two hands
Simplified

3rd finger left hand

S W S (space)

Say the letters and spaces as you work

Make a block of this group of letters like this:

SWS SWS SWS SWS SWS SWS SWS
SWS SWS SWS SWS SWS SWS SWS
SWS SWS SWS SWS SWS SWS SWS
SWS SWS SWS SWS SWS SWS SWS
SWS SWS SWS SWS SWS SWS SWS
SWS SWS SWS SWS SWS SWS SWS

Word processing with two hands
Simplified

3rd finger left hand

S X S (space)

Say the letters and spaces as you work

Make a block of this group of letters like this:

SXS SXS SXS SXS SXS SXS SXS
SXS SXS SXS SXS SXS SXS SXS
SXS SXS SXS SXS SXS SXS SXS
SXS SXS SXS SXS SXS SXS SXS
SXS SXS SXS SXS SXS SXS SXS
SXS SXS SXS SXS SXS SXS SXS

Word processing with two hands
Simplified

3rd finger right hand

l o l (space)

Say the letters and spaces as you work

Make a block of this group of letters like this:

lol lol lol lol lol lol lol
lol lol lol lol lol lol lol
lol lol lol lol lol lol lol
lol lol lol lol lol lol lol
lol lol lol lol lol lol lol
lol lol lol lol lol lol lol

Word processing with two hands
Simplified

3rd finger right hand

1 . 1 (space)

Say the letters and spaces as you work

Make a block of this group of letters like this:

1.1 1.1 1.1 1.1 1.1 1.1 1.1
1.1 1.1 1.1 1.1 1.1 1.1 1.1
1.1 1.1 1.1 1.1 1.1 1.1 1.1
1.1 1.1 1.1 1.1 1.1 1.1 1.1
1.1 1.1 1.1 1.1 1.1 1.1 1.1
1.1 1.1 1.1 1.1 1.1 1.1 1.1

Word processing with two hands
Simplified

4th finger left hand

a q a (space)

Say the letters and spaces as you work

Make a block of this group of letters like this:

aqa aqa aqa aqa aqa aqa aqa
aqa aqa aqa aqa aqa aqa aqa
aqa aqa aqa aqa aqa aqa aqa
aqa aqa aqa aqa aqa aqa aqa
aqa aqa aqa aqa aqa aqa aqa
aqa aqa aqa aqa aqa aqa aqa

Word processing with two hands
Simplified

4th finger left hand

a z a (space)

Say the letters and spaces as you work

Make a block of this group of letters like this:

aza aza aza aza aza aza aza
aza aza aza aza aza aza aza
aza aza aza aza aza aza aza
aza aza aza aza aza aza aza
aza aza aza aza aza aza aza
aza aza aza aza aza aza aza

Word processing with two hands
Simplified

4th finger right hand

; p ; (space)

Say the letters and spaces as you work

Make a block of this group of letters like this:

;p; ;p; ;p; ;p; ;p; ;p; ;p;
;p; ;p; ;p; ;p; ;p; ;p; ;p;
;p; ;p; ;p; ;p; ;p; ;p; ;p;
;p; ;p; ;p; ;p; ;p; ;p; ;p;
;p; ;p; ;p; ;p; ;p; ;p; ;p;
;p; ;p; ;p; ;p; ;p; ;p; ;p;

Word processing with two hands
Simplified

4th finger right hand

; / ;   (space)

Say the letters and spaces as you work

Make a block of this group of letters like this:

;/; ;/; ;/; ;/; ;/; ;/; ;/;
;/; ;/; ;/; ;/; ;/; ;/; ;/;
;/; ;/; ;/; ;/; ;/; ;/; ;/;
;/; ;/; ;/; ;/; ;/; ;/; ;/;
;/; ;/; ;/; ;/; ;/; ;/; ;/;
;/; ;/; ;/; ;/; ;/; ;/; ;/;

Word processing with two hands

When you have practised worksheets 1–5, try these words. You will need to use your 1st fingers and your left or right thumb for the space bar

fur   rug   mug
hug   gum   hum

Say the letters and spaces as you work

Make a block of each of the words

fur fur fur fur fur fur fur
fur fur fur fur fur fur fur
fur fur fur fur fur fur fur
fur fur fur fur fur fur fur
fur fur fur fur fur fur fur
fur fur fur fur fur fur fur

Word processing with two hands

When you have practised worksheets 1–7, try these words.
You will need to use your 1st fingers and your left or right
thumb for the space bar

but   run   my

nut   fun   hut

Say the letters and spaces as you work

Make a block of each of the words

but but but but but but but
but but but but but but but
but but but but but but but
but but but but but but but
but but but but but but but
but but but but but but but

Word processing with two hands

When you have practised worksheets 1–7, try these words.
You will need to use your 1st fingers and your left or right
thumb for the space bar

by   try   hurry
turn bun thumb

Say the letters and spaces as you work

Make a block of each of the words

turn turn turn turn turn turn
turn turn turn turn turn turn
turn turn turn turn turn turn
turn turn turn turn turn turn
turn turn turn turn turn turn
turn turn turn turn turn turn

Word processing with two hands

When you have practised worksheets 1–9, try these words.
You will need to use your 1st and 2nd fingers and your left or
right thumb for the space bar

neck under tidy
the number very

Say the letters and spaces as you work

Make a block of each of the words

very very very very very very
very very very very very very
very very very very very very
very very very very very very
very very very very very very
very very very very very very

Word processing with two hands

When you have practised worksheets 1–11, try these words.
You will need to use your 1st, 2nd and 3rd fingers and your
left or right thumb for the space bar

sweet chest little
will   good   next

Say the letters and spaces as you work

Make a block of each of the words

little little little little little
little little little little little
little little little little little
little little little little little
little little little little little
little little little little little

Word processing with two hands

When you have practised worksheets 1–13, try these words.
You will need to use your 1st, 2nd 3rd and 4th fingers and
your left or right thumb for the space bar

queen zoo pretty
and have speed

Say the letters and spaces as you work

Make a block of each of the words

have have have have have
have have have have have
have have have have have
have have have have have
have have have have have
have have have have have

Word processing with the right hand

Home keys

1st finger	2nd finger	3rd finger	4th finger
f	g	h	j

Always begin with your fingers over these keys

Your thumb will be ready to use the space bar

Word processing with the right hand

1st finger

f r f v f (space)

Say the letters and spaces as you work

Make a block of this group of letters like this:

frfvf frfvf frfvf frfvf frfvf frfvf
frfvf frfvf frfvf frfvf frfvf frfvf
frfvf frfvf frfvf frfvf frfvf frfvf
frfvf frfvf frfvf frfvf frfvf frfvf
frfvf frfvf frfvf frfvf frfvf frfvf
frfvf frfvf frfvf frfvf frfvf frfvf

Word processing with the right hand

2nd finger

g t g b g (space)

Say the letters and spaces as you work

Make a block of this group of letters like this:

gtgbg gtgbg gtgbg gtgbg gtgbg
gtgbg gtgbg gtgbg gtgbg gtgbg
gtgbg gtgbg gtgbg gtgbg gtgbg
gtgbg gtgbg gtgbg gtgbg gtgbg
gtgbg gtgbg gtgbg gtgbg gtgbg
gtgbg gtgbg gtgbg gtgbg gtgbg

Word processing with the right hand

3rd finger

h y h n h (space)

Say the letters and spaces as you work

Make a block of this group of letters like this:

hyhnh hyhnh hyhnh hyhnh hyhnh
hyhnh hyhnh hyhnh hyhnh hyhnh
hyhnh hyhnh hyhnh hyhnh hyhnh
hyhnh hyhnh hyhnh hyhnh hyhnh
hyhnh hyhnh hyhnh hyhnh hyhnh
hyhnh hyhnh hyhnh hyhnh hyhnh

Word processing with the right hand

4th finger

j u j m j (space)

Say the letters and spaces as you work

Make a block of this group of letters like this:

jujmj jujmj jujmj jujmj jujmj
jujmj jujmj jujmj jujmj jujmj
jujmj jujmj jujmj jujmj jujmj
jujmj jujmj jujmj jujmj jujmj
jujmj jujmj jujmj jujmj jujmj
jujmj jujmj jujmj jujmj jujmj

Word processing with the right hand

1st finger

d e d c d (space)

Say the letters and spaces as you work

Make a block of this group of letters like this:

dedcd dedcd dedcd dedcd dedcd
dedcd dedcd dedcd dedcd dedcd
dedcd dedcd dedcd dedcd dedcd
dedcd dedcd dedcd dedcd dedcd
dedcd dedcd dedcd dedcd dedcd
dedcd dedcd dedcd dedcd dedcd

Word processing with the right hand

1st finger

S W S X S (space)

Say the letters and spaces as you work

Make a block of this group of letters like this:

SWSXS SWSXS SWSXS SWSXS SWSXS
SWSXS SWSXS SWSXS SWSXS SWSXS
SWSXS SWSXS SWSXS SWSXS SWSXS
SWSXS SWSXS SWSXS SWSXS SWSXS
SWSXS SWSXS SWSXS SWSXS SWSXS
SWSXS SWSXS SWSXS SWSXS SWSXS

Word processing with the right hand

1st finger

a q a z a (space)

Say the letters and spaces as you work

Make a block of this group of letters like this:

aqaza aqaza aqaza aqaza aqaza
aqaza aqaza aqaza aqaza aqaza
aqaza aqaza aqaza aqaza aqaza
aqaza aqaza aqaza aqaza aqaza
aqaza aqaza aqaza aqaza aqaza
aqaza aqaza aqaza aqaza aqaza

Word processing with the right hand

4th finger

kik, k (space)

Say the letters and spaces as you work

Make a block of this group of letters like this:

kik,k kik,k kik,k kik,k kik,k
kik,k kik,k kik,k kik,k kik,k
kik,k kik,k kik,k kik,k kik,k
kik,k kik,k kik,k kik,k kik,k
kik,k kik,k kik,k kik,k kik,k
kik,k kik,k kik,k kik,k kik,k

Word processing with the right hand

4th finger

l o l . l (space)

Say the letters and spaces as you work

Make a block of this group of letters like this:

lol.l lol.l lol.l lol.l lol.l
lol.l lol.l lol.l lol.l lol.l
lol.l lol.l lol.l lol.l lol.l
lol.l lol.l lol.l lol.l lol.l
lol.l lol.l lol.l lol.l lol.l
lol.l lol.l lol.l lol.l lol.l

Word processing with the right hand

4th finger

; p ; / ; (space)

Say the letters and spaces as you work

Make a block of this group of letters like this:

;p;/; ;p;/; ;p;/; ;p;/; ;p;/;
;p;/; ;p;/; ;p;/; ;p;/; ;p;/;
;p;/; ;p;/; ;p;/; ;p;/; ;p;/;
;p;/; ;p;/; ;p;/; ;p;/; ;p;/;
;p;/; ;p;/; ;p;/; ;p;/; ;p;/;
;p;/; ;p;/; ;p;/; ;p;/; ;p;/;

Word processing with the right hand
Simplified

1st finger

frf (space)

Say the letters and spaces as you work

Make a block of this group of letters like this:

frf frf frf frf frf frf frf
frf frf frf frf frf frf frf
frf frf frf frf frf frf frf
frf frf frf frf frf frf frf
frf frf frf frf frf frf frf
frf frf frf frf frf frf frf

Word processing with the right hand
Simplified

1st finger

f v f (space)

Say the letters and spaces as you work

Make a block of this group of letters like this:

fvf fvf fvf fvf fvf fvf
fvf fvf fvf fvf fvf fvf
fvf fvf fvf fvf fvf fvf
fvf fvf fvf fvf fvf fvf
fvf fvf fvf fvf fvf fvf
fvf fvf fvf fvf fvf fvf

Worksheet 55

Word processing with the right hand
Simplified

2nd finger

g t g (space)

Say the letters and spaces as you work

Make a block of this group of letters like this:

gtg gtg gtg gtg gtg gtg
gtg gtg gtg gtg gtg gtg
gtg gtg gtg gtg gtg gtg
gtg gtg gtg gtg gtg gtg
gtg gtg gtg gtg gtg gtg
gtg gtg gtg gtg gtg gtg

Worksheet 56

Word processing with the right hand
Simplified

2nd finger

g b g (space)

Say the letters and spaces as you work

Make a block of this group of letters like this:

gbg gbg gbg gbg gbg gbg
gbg gbg gbg gbg gbg gbg
gbg gbg gbg gbg gbg gbg
gbg gbg gbg gbg gbg gbg
gbg gbg gbg gbg gbg gbg
gbg gbg gbg gbg gbg gbg

Word processing with the right hand
Simplified

3rd finger

h y h (space)

Say the letters and spaces as you work

Make a block of this group of letters like this:

hyh hyh hyh hyh hyh hyh
hyh hyh hyh hyh hyh hyh
hyh hyh hyh hyh hyh hyh
hyh hyh hyh hyh hyh hyh
hyh hyh hyh hyh hyh hyh
hyh hyh hyh hyh hyh hyh

Word processing with the right hand
Simplified

3rd finger

h n h (space)

Say the letters and spaces as you work

Make a block of this group of letters like this:

hnh hnh hnh hnh hnh hnh
hnh hnh hnh hnh hnh hnh
hnh hnh hnh hnh hnh hnh
hnh hnh hnh hnh hnh hnh
hnh hnh hnh hnh hnh hnh
hnh hnh hnh hnh hnh hnh

Word processing with the right hand
Simplified

4th finger

j u j (space)

Say the letters and spaces as you work

Make a block of this group of letters like this:

juj juj juj juj juj juj
juj juj juj juj juj juj
juj juj juj juj juj juj
juj juj juj juj juj juj
juj juj juj juj juj juj
juj juj juj juj juj juj

Word processing with the right hand
Simplified

4th finger

j m j (space)

Say the letters and spaces as you work

Make a block of this group of letters like this:

jmj jmj jmj jmj jmj jmj
jmj jmj jmj jmj jmj jmj
jmj jmj jmj jmj jmj jmj
jmj jmj jmj jmj jmj jmj
jmj jmj jmj jmj jmj jmj
jmj jmj jmj jmj jmj jmj

Worksheet 61

Word processing with the right hand
Simplified

1st finger

d e d (space)

Say the letters and spaces as you work

Make a block of this group of letters like this:

ded ded ded ded ded ded ded
ded ded ded ded ded ded ded
ded ded ded ded ded ded ded
ded ded ded ded ded ded ded
ded ded ded ded ded ded ded
ded ded ded ded ded ded ded

Word processing with the right hand
Simplified

1st finger

d c d (space)

Say the letters and spaces as you work

Make a block of this group of letters like this:

dcd dcd dcd dcd dcd dcd dcd
dcd dcd dcd dcd dcd dcd dcd
dcd dcd dcd dcd dcd dcd dcd
dcd dcd dcd dcd dcd dcd dcd
dcd dcd dcd dcd dcd dcd dcd
dcd dcd dcd dcd dcd dcd dcd

Word processing with the right hand
Simplified

4th finger

k i k (space)

Say the letters and spaces as you work

Make a block of this group of letters like this:

kik kik kik kik kik kik kik
kik kik kik kik kik kik kik
kik kik kik kik kik kik kik
kik kik kik kik kik kik kik
kik kik kik kik kik kik kik
kik kik kik kik kik kik kik

Word processing with two hands
Simplified

4th finger

k , k (space)

Say the letters and spaces as you work

Make a block of this group of letters like this:

k,k k,k k,k k,k k,k k,k k,k
k,k k,k k,k k,k k,k k,k k,k
k,k k,k k,k k,k k,k k,k k,k
k,k k,k k,k k,k k,k k,k k,k
k,k k,k k,k k,k k,k k,k k,k
k,k k,k k,k k,k k,k k,k k,k

Word processing with two hands
Simplified

1st finger

S W S (space)

Say the letters and spaces as you work

Make a block of this group of letters like this:

SWS SWS SWS SWS SWS SWS SWS
SWS SWS SWS SWS SWS SWS SWS
SWS SWS SWS SWS SWS SWS SWS
SWS SWS SWS SWS SWS SWS SWS
SWS SWS SWS SWS SWS SWS SWS
SWS SWS SWS SWS SWS SWS SWS

Word processing with the right hand
Simplified

1st finger

S X S (space)

Say the letters and spaces as you work

Make a block of this group of letters like this:

SXS SXS SXS SXS SXS SXS SXS

SXS SXS SXS SXS SXS SXS SXS

SXS SXS SXS SXS SXS SXS SXS

SXS SXS SXS SXS SXS SXS SXS

SXS SXS SXS SXS SXS SXS SXS

SXS SXS SXS SXS SXS SXS SXS

Word processing with the right hand
Simplified

4th finger

l o l (space)

Say the letters and spaces as you work

Make a block of this group of letters like this:

lol lol lol lol lol lol lol
lol lol lol lol lol lol lol
lol lol lol lol lol lol lol
lol lol lol lol lol lol lol
lol lol lol lol lol lol lol
lol lol lol lol lol lol lol

Word processing with the right hand
Simplified

4th finger

1.1 (space)

Say the letters and spaces as you work

Make a block of this group of letters like this:

1.1 1.1 1.1 1.1 1.1 1.1 1.1
1.1 1.1 1.1 1.1 1.1 1.1 1.1
1.1 1.1 1.1 1.1 1.1 1.1 1.1
1.1 1.1 1.1 1.1 1.1 1.1 1.1
1.1 1.1 1.1 1.1 1.1 1.1 1.1
1.1 1.1 1.1 1.1 1.1 1.1 1.1

Worksheet 69

Word processing with the right hand
Simplified

1st finger

a q a (space)

Say the letters and spaces as you work

Make a block of this group of letters like this:

aqa aqa aqa aqa aqa aqa aqa
aqa aqa aqa aqa aqa aqa aqa
aqa aqa aqa aqa aqa aqa aqa
aqa aqa aqa aqa aqa aqa aqa
aqa aqa aqa aqa aqa aqa aqa
aqa aqa aqa aqa aqa aqa aqa

Word processing with the right hand
Simplified

1st finger

a z a (space)

Say the letters and spaces as you work

Make a block of this group of letters like this:

aza aza aza aza aza aza aza
aza aza aza aza aza aza aza
aza aza aza aza aza aza aza
aza aza aza aza aza aza aza
aza aza aza aza aza aza aza
aza aza aza aza aza aza aza

Word processing with the right hand
Simplified

4th finger

Say the letters and spaces as you work

Make a block of this group of letters like this:

;p; ;p; ;p; ;p; ;p; ;p; ;p;
;p; ;p; ;p; ;p; ;p; ;p; ;p;
;p; ;p; ;p; ;p; ;p; ;p; ;p;
;p; ;p; ;p; ;p; ;p; ;p; ;p;
;p; ;p; ;p; ;p; ;p; ;p; ;p;
;p; ;p; ;p; ;p; ;p; ;p; ;p;

Word processing with the right hand
Simplified

4th finger

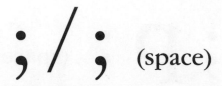

; / ; (space)

Say the letters and spaces as you work

Make a block of this group of letters like this:

;/; ;/; ;/; ;/; ;/; ;/; ;/;
;/; ;/; ;/; ;/; ;/; ;/; ;/;
;/; ;/; ;/; ;/; ;/; ;/; ;/;
;/; ;/; ;/; ;/; ;/; ;/; ;/;
;/; ;/; ;/; ;/; ;/; ;/; ;/;
;/; ;/; ;/; ;/; ;/; ;/; ;/;

Word processing with the left hand

Home keys

4th finger	3rd finger	2nd finger	1st finger
f	**g**	**h**	**j**

Always begin with your fingers over these keys

Your thumb will be ready to use the space bar

Word processing with the left hand

1st finger

j u j m j (space)

Say the letters and spaces as you work

Make a block of this group of letters like this:

jujmj jujmj jujmj jujmj jujmj
jujmj jujmj jujmj jujmj jujmj
jujmj jujmj jujmj jujmj jujmj
jujmj jujmj jujmj jujmj jujmj
jujmj jujmj jujmj jujmj jujmj
jujmj jujmj jujmj jujmj jujmj

Word processing with the left hand

2nd finger

h y h n h (space)

Say the letters and spaces as you work

Make a block of this group of letters like this:

hyhnh hyhnh hyhnh hyhnh hyhnh
hyhnh hyhnh hyhnh hyhnh hyhnh
hyhnh hyhnh hyhnh hyhnh hyhnh
hyhnh hyhnh hyhnh hyhnh hyhnh
hyhnh hyhnh hyhnh hyhnh hyhnh
hyhnh hyhnh hyhnh hyhnh hyhnh

Worksheet 76

Word processing with the left hand

3rd finger

g t g b g (space)

Say the letters and spaces as you work

Make a block of this group of letters like this:

gtgbg gtgbg gtgbg gtgbg gtgbg
gtgbg gtgbg gtgbg gtgbg gtgbg
gtgbg gtgbg gtgbg gtgbg gtgbg
gtgbg gtgbg gtgbg gtgbg gtgbg
gtgbg gtgbg gtgbg gtgbg gtgbg
gtgbg gtgbg gtgbg gtgbg gtgbg

Word processing with the left hand

4th finger

f r f v f (space)

Say the letters and spaces as you work

Make a block of this group of letters like this:

frfvf frfvf frfvf frfvf frfvf frfvf
frfvf frfvf frfvf frfvf frfvf frfvf
frfvf frfvf frfvf frfvf frfvf frfvf
frfvf frfvf frfvf frfvf frfvf frfvf
frfvf frfvf frfvf frfvf frfvf frfvf
frfvf frfvf frfvf frfvf frfvf frfvf

Word processing with the left hand

1st finger

kik,k (space)

Say the letters and spaces as you work

Make a block of this group of letters like this:

kik,k kik,k kik,k kik,k kik,k
kik,k kik,k kik,k kik,k kik,k
kik,k kik,k kik,k kik,k kik,k
kik,k kik,k kik,k kik,k kik,k
kik,k kik,k kik,k kik,k kik,k
kik,k kik,k kik,k kik,k kik,k

Word processing with the left hand

1st finger

l o l . l (space)

Say the letters and spaces as you work

Make a block of this group of letters like this:

lol.l lol.l lol.l lol.l lol.l
lol.l lol.l lol.l lol.l lol.l
lol.l lol.l lol.l lol.l lol.l
lol.l lol.l lol.l lol.l lol.l
lol.l lol.l lol.l lol.l lol.l
lol.l lol.l lol.l lol.l lol.l

Worksheet 80

Word processing with the left hand

1st finger

; p ; / ; (space)

Say the letters and spaces as you work

Make a block of this group of letters like this:

;p;/; ;p;/; ;p;/; ;p;/; ;p;/;
;p;/; ;p;/; ;p;/; ;p;/; ;p;/;
;p;/; ;p;/; ;p;/; ;p;/; ;p;/;
;p;/; ;p;/; ;p;/; ;p;/; ;p;/;
;p;/; ;p;/; ;p;/; ;p;/; ;p;/;
;p;/; ;p;/; ;p;/; ;p;/; ;p;/;

Worksheet 81

Word processing with the left hand

4th finger

d e d c d (space)

Say the letters and spaces as you work

Make a block of this group of letters like this:

dedcd dedcd dedcd dedcd dedcd
dedcd dedcd dedcd dedcd dedcd
dedcd dedcd dedcd dedcd dedcd
dedcd dedcd dedcd dedcd dedcd
dedcd dedcd dedcd dedcd dedcd
dedcd dedcd dedcd dedcd dedcd

Word processing with the left hand

4th finger

S W S X S (space)

Say the letters and spaces as you work

Make a block of this group of letters like this:

SWSXS SWSXS SWSXS SWSXS SWSXS
SWSXS SWSXS SWSXS SWSXS SWSXS
SWSXS SWSXS SWSXS SWSXS SWSXS
SWSXS SWSXS SWSXS SWSXS SWSXS
SWSXS SWSXS SWSXS SWSXS SWSXS
SWSXS SWSXS SWSXS SWSXS SWSXS

Word processing with the left hand

4th finger

a q a z a (space)

Say the letters and spaces as you work

Make a block of this group of letters like this:

aqaza aqaza aqaza aqaza aqaza
aqaza aqaza aqaza aqaza aqaza
aqaza aqaza aqaza aqaza aqaza
aqaza aqaza aqaza aqaza aqaza
aqaza aqaza aqaza aqaza aqaza
aqaza aqaza aqaza aqaza aqaza

Word processing with the left hand
Simplified

1st finger

j u j (space)

Say the letters and spaces as you work

Make a block of this group of letters like this:

juj juj juj juj juj juj
juj juj juj juj juj juj
juj juj juj juj juj juj
juj juj juj juj juj juj
juj juj juj juj juj juj
juj juj juj juj juj juj

Worksheet 85

Word processing with the left hand
Simplified

1st finger

j m j (space)

Say the letters and spaces as you work

Make a block of this group of letters like this:

jmj jmj jmj jmj jmj jmj
jmj jmj jmj jmj jmj jmj
jmj jmj jmj jmj jmj jmj
jmj jmj jmj jmj jmj jmj
jmj jmj jmj jmj jmj jmj
jmj jmj jmj jmj jmj jmj

Word processing with the left hand
Simplified

2nd finger

h y h (space)

Say the letters and spaces as you work

Make a block of this group of letters like this:

hyh hyh hyh hyh hyh hyh
hyh hyh hyh hyh hyh hyh
hyh hyh hyh hyh hyh hyh
hyh hyh hyh hyh hyh hyh
hyh hyh hyh hyh hyh hyh
hyh hyh hyh hyh hyh hyh

Worksheet 87

Word processing with the left hand
Simplified

2nd finger

h n h (space)

Say the letters and spaces as you work

Make a block of this group of letters like this:

hnh hnh hnh hnh hnh hnh
hnh hnh hnh hnh hnh hnh
hnh hnh hnh hnh hnh hnh
hnh hnh hnh hnh hnh hnh
hnh hnh hnh hnh hnh hnh
hnh hnh hnh hnh hnh hnh

Worksheet 88

Word processing with the left hand
Simplified

3rd finger

g t g (space)

Say the letters and spaces as you work

Make a block of this group of letters like this:

gtg gtg gtg gtg gtg gtg
gtg gtg gtg gtg gtg gtg
gtg gtg gtg gtg gtg gtg
gtg gtg gtg gtg gtg gtg
gtg gtg gtg gtg gtg gtg
gtg gtg gtg gtg gtg gtg

Worksheet 89

Word processing with the left hand
Simplified

3rd finger

g b g (space)

Say the letters and spaces as you work

Make a block of this group of letters like this:

gbg gbg gbg gbg gbg gbg
gbg gbg gbg gbg gbg gbg
gbg gbg gbg gbg gbg gbg
gbg gbg gbg gbg gbg gbg
gbg gbg gbg gbg gbg gbg
gbg gbg gbg gbg gbg gbg

Word processing with the left hand
Simplified

4th finger

f r f (space)

Say the letters and spaces as you work

Make a block of this group of letters like this:

frf frf frf frf frf frf frf
frf frf frf frf frf frf frf
frf frf frf frf frf frf frf
frf frf frf frf frf frf frf
frf frf frf frf frf frf frf
frf frf frf frf frf frf frf

Word processing with the left hand
Simplified

4th finger

fvf (space)

Say the letters and spaces as you work

Make a block of this group of letters like this:

fvf fvf fvf fvf fvf fvf
fvf fvf fvf fvf fvf fvf
fvf fvf fvf fvf fvf fvf
fvf fvf fvf fvf fvf fvf
fvf fvf fvf fvf fvf fvf
fvf fvf fvf fvf fvf fvf

Word processing with the left hand
Simplified

4th finger

d e d (space)

Say the letters and spaces as you work

Make a block of this group of letters like this:

ded ded ded ded ded ded ded
ded ded ded ded ded ded ded
ded ded ded ded ded ded ded
ded ded ded ded ded ded ded
ded ded ded ded ded ded ded
ded ded ded ded ded ded ded

Word processing with the left hand
Simplified

4th finger

d c d (space)

Say the letters and spaces as you work

Make a block of this group of letters like this:

dcd dcd dcd dcd dcd dcd dcd
dcd dcd dcd dcd dcd dcd dcd
dcd dcd dcd dcd dcd dcd dcd
dcd dcd dcd dcd dcd dcd dcd
dcd dcd dcd dcd dcd dcd dcd
dcd dcd dcd dcd dcd dcd dcd

Word processing with the left hand
Simplified

1st finger

kik (space)

Say the letters and spaces as you work

Make a block of this group of letters like this:

kik kik kik kik kik kik kik
kik kik kik kik kik kik kik
kik kik kik kik kik kik kik
kik kik kik kik kik kik kik
kik kik kik kik kik kik kik
kik kik kik kik kik kik kik

Word processing with the left hand
Simplified

1st finger

k , k (space)

Say the letters and spaces as you work

Make a block of this group of letters like this:

k,k k,k k,k k,k k,k k,k k,k
k,k k,k k,k k,k k,k k,k k,k
k,k k,k k,k k,k k,k k,k k,k
k,k k,k k,k k,k k,k k,k k,k
k,k k,k k,k k,k k,k k,k k,k
k,k k,k k,k k,k k,k k,k k,k

Word processing with the left hand
Simplified

4th finger

S W S (space)

Say the letters and spaces as you work

Make a block of this group of letters like this:

SWS SWS SWS SWS SWS SWS SWS
SWS SWS SWS SWS SWS SWS SWS
SWS SWS SWS SWS SWS SWS SWS
SWS SWS SWS SWS SWS SWS SWS
SWS SWS SWS SWS SWS SWS SWS
SWS SWS SWS SWS SWS SWS SWS

Word processing with the left hand
Simplified

4th finger

S X S (space)

Say the letters and spaces as you work

Make a block of this group of letters like this:

SXS SXS SXS SXS SXS SXS SXS

SXS SXS SXS SXS SXS SXS SXS

SXS SXS SXS SXS SXS SXS SXS

SXS SXS SXS SXS SXS SXS SXS

SXS SXS SXS SXS SXS SXS SXS

SXS SXS SXS SXS SXS SXS SXS

Word processing with the left hand
Simplified

1st finger

l o l (space)

Say the letters and spaces as you work

Make a block of this group of letters like this:

lol lol lol lol lol lol lol
lol lol lol lol lol lol lol
lol lol lol lol lol lol lol
lol lol lol lol lol lol lol
lol lol lol lol lol lol lol
lol lol lol lol lol lol lol

Worksheet 99

Word processing with the left hand
Simplified

1st finger

1.1 (space)

Say the letters and spaces as you work

Make a block of this group of letters like this:

1.1 1.1 1.1 1.1 1.1 1.1 1.1
1.1 1.1 1.1 1.1 1.1 1.1 1.1
1.1 1.1 1.1 1.1 1.1 1.1 1.1
1.1 1.1 1.1 1.1 1.1 1.1 1.1
1.1 1.1 1.1 1.1 1.1 1.1 1.1
1.1 1.1 1.1 1.1 1.1 1.1 1.1

Word processing with the left hand
Simplified

4th finger

a q a (space)

Say the letters and spaces as you work

Make a block of this group of letters like this:

aqa aqa aqa aqa aqa aqa aqa
aqa aqa aqa aqa aqa aqa aqa
aqa aqa aqa aqa aqa aqa aqa
aqa aqa aqa aqa aqa aqa aqa
aqa aqa aqa aqa aqa aqa aqa
aqa aqa aqa aqa aqa aqa aqa

Worksheet 101

Word processing with the left hand
Simplified

4th finger

a z a (space)

Say the letters and spaces as you work

Make a block of this group of letters like this:

aza aza aza aza aza aza aza
aza aza aza aza aza aza aza
aza aza aza aza aza aza aza
aza aza aza aza aza aza aza
aza aza aza aza aza aza aza
aza aza aza aza aza aza aza

Word processing with the left hand
Simplified

1st finger

; p ; (space)

Say the letters and spaces as you work

Make a block of this group of letters like this:

;p; ;p; ;p; ;p; ;p; ;p; ;p;
;p; ;p; ;p; ;p; ;p; ;p; ;p;
;p; ;p; ;p; ;p; ;p; ;p; ;p;
;p; ;p; ;p; ;p; ;p; ;p; ;p;
;p; ;p; ;p; ;p; ;p; ;p; ;p;
;p; ;p; ;p; ;p; ;p; ;p; ;p;

Word processing with the left hand
Simplified

1st finger

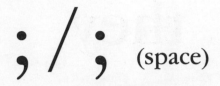

; / ;   (space)

Say the letters and spaces as you work

Make a block of this group of letters like this:

;/; ;/; ;/; ;/; ;/; ;/; ;/;
;/; ;/; ;/; ;/; ;/; ;/; ;/;
;/; ;/; ;/; ;/; ;/; ;/; ;/;
;/; ;/; ;/; ;/; ;/; ;/; ;/;
;/; ;/; ;/; ;/; ;/; ;/; ;/;
;/; ;/; ;/; ;/; ;/; ;/; ;/;

Word processing – words that are used often

Practise these words – you will use them often

the they then

them there

we went were

a an and are

Say the letters and spaces as you work

Make a block of each of the words:

the the the the the
the the the the the
the the the the the
the the the the the
the the the the the

Worksheet 105

Word processing – words that use adjacent keys

Especially useful practice for one-handed word processing

Look at the pattern the letters make on the keyboard

pool loop look
oil milk you

Say the letters and spaces as you work

Make a block of each of the words:

look look look look look
look look look look look
look look look look look
look look look look look
look look look look look

Word processing – words that use adjacent keys

Especially useful practice for one-handed word processing.

Look at the pattern the letters make on the keyboard

was   red   seed
were   deer   sad

Say the letters and spaces as you work

Make a block of each of the words:

was was was was was was
was was was was was was
was was was was was was
was was was was was was
was was was was was was
was was was was was was

Words that require big stretches when word processing with one hand

Look where the letters are on the keyboard

Work out how you will need to move your hand

apple paw deep
peel zip leap

Say the letters and spaces as you work

Make a block of each of the words:

apple apple apple apple apple
apple apple apple apple apple
apple apple apple apple apple
apple apple apple appleapple
apple apple apple apple apple
apple apple apple apple apple

Words that require big stretches when word processing with one hand

Look where the letters are on the keyboard

Work out how you will need to move your hand

view new drop supper play last

Say the letters and spaces as you work

Make a block of each of the words:

play play play play play play
play play play play play play
play play play play play play
play play play play play play
play play play play play play
play play play play play play

Worksheet 109

Word processing – capital letters

Press the shift key with your 4th finger on the side of the keyboard opposite to where you will fire the key

Monday

Press the left shift key with the 4th finger of your left hand, fire 'M', release shift key

Sunday

Press the right shift key with the 4th finger of your right hand, fire 'S', release shift key

Now try your name and the names of people in your family and your friends

As you work say, 'shift, letter, release shift'

Word processing – capital letters

Try your name and address
Copy it if you are not sure how to spell the words
Remember that each word will need a capital letter

Do you know the names of any countries?

England France
Germany Italy Spain
United States of America

Say the shift, letters and spaces as you work

Make a block of each word:

England England England England
England England England England
England England England England

Word processing – words and letter strings

Choose one letter from the left side of the page
Add a group of letters from across the top of the page

What is the word you have made?

ill   it   at

b

f

h

s

Word processing – words and letter strings

Choose one letter from the left side of the page
Add a group of letters from across the top of the page

What is the word you have made?

ash   **ace**   **ate**

d

l

m

r

Word processing – letter strings

Practise these letter strings, then see if you can put each one into a word

tion   ing   able   ible

ent   ist   est   ere

ed   ally   ery   ange

ies   ough   ence   ance

ead   ace   ouch   ity

Word processing – sound blends

Practise these sound blends then put each one into a word

bl br ch chr cl cr dr fl fr gl gr pl pr sh shr sl sp spr st str sw sm sn th thr tr

Worksheet 115

Word processing – completing sentences

Copy these sentences putting in the missing words

I am _____ years old.

I like _____.

I live with _____.

My favourite food is _____.

On Saturday I usually _____.

Word processing — completing sentences

Copy these sentences putting in the missing words

Snow usually falls in ——————————.

Daffodils flower in ——————————.

Some trees lose their leaves in ————————.

The warmest part of the year is————————.

Word processing — completing sentences

Copy these sentences putting in the missing words

Red paint mixed with blue paint makes _____ .

Blue paint mixed with yellow paint makes _____ .

Red paint mixed with yellow paint makes _____ .

Word processing – fingering when using both hands

Fill in the keys that will be fired by each finger

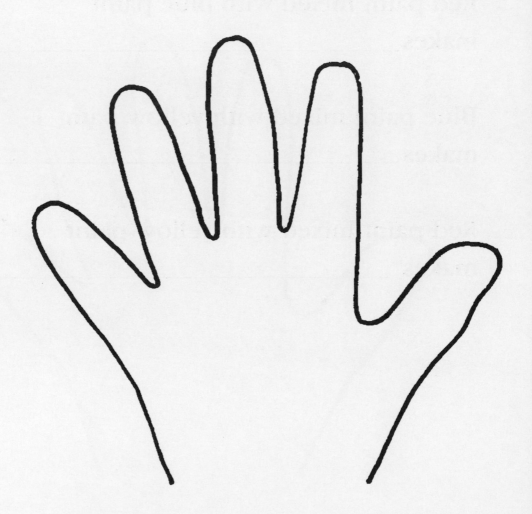

Word processing – fingering when using both hands

Fill in the keys that will be fired by each finger

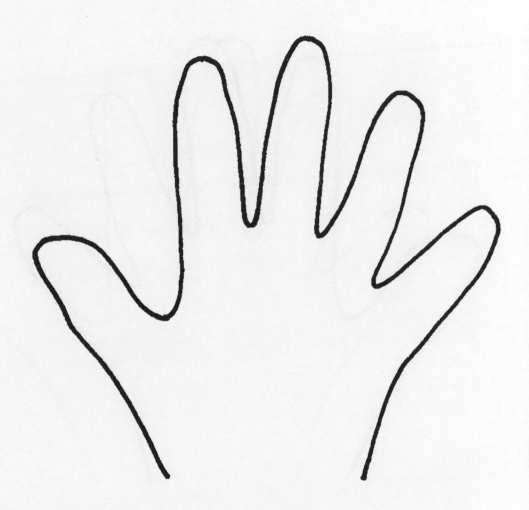

Word processing – fingering when using the right hand

Fill in the keys that will be fired by each finger

Word processing – fingering when using the left hand

Fill in the keys that will be fired by each finger

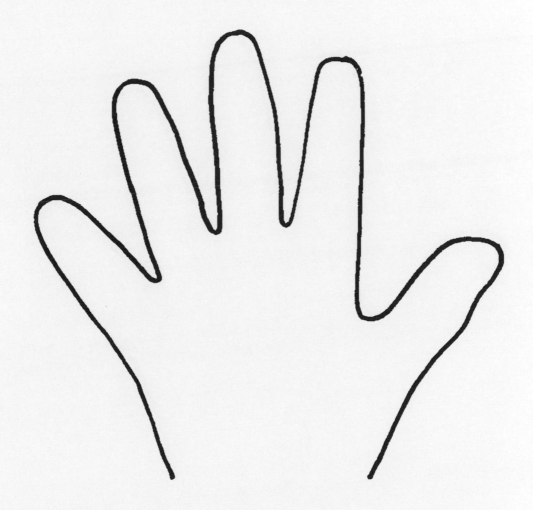

Index

achondroplasia 24
amniotic bands 25
arm rests *see* rests for arms or wrists
arthrogryposis 23–24
Asperger's syndrome 13–14
ataxia 17
athetosis 17–18
attention deficit disorder 14, 34
attention deficit hyperactivity disorder
    14, 34

behavioural problems 14–15
benign essential tremor *see* tremor
brittle bones *see* osteogenesis imperfecta

capital letters *see* upper case letters
colour blindness 9
colour coding 76

developmental co-ordination disorder
    see perceptuo motor difficulties
diplegia 19
drooling 20, 50
Dvorak keyboards *see* keyboards, Dvorak
dyslexia 12–13
dyspraxia *see* motor planning
dystonia 21
    musculorum deformans 21

educational needs 66–68
emotional problems *see* behavioural
    problems
epilepsy 14
ergonomic keyboards *see* keyboards,
    ergonomic
expanded keyboards *see* keyboards,
    expanded

fine motor skills 31–33
Friedreich's ataxia 17

hand function *see* fine motor skills
hand injuries 23
hand skills *see* fine motor skills
hearing impairment 10
hemiplegia 9, 18, 55
home keys 75, 77
    worksheets 1, 42, 73 98–99, 140, 171

juvenile chronic arthritis 22–23

keyboarding skills
    advantages of using 71–72
    importance of learning 3, 72
    teaching methods 4, 72–80
keyboards 39–46
    size of 40–42
    angle of 42
    the keys 42–43
    expanded 43–44
    ergonomic 44–45
    Dvorak 45–46
keyboard gloves or skins 49–50
keyguards 46–47

lighting 74
limb deficiency 24
lower case letters 51

mobility 29–31
monitor 51–57
    angle of 54–55
    contrast 53–54
    resolution 53
    size of 52–53
Morquio's syndrome 23
motivation 35, 68–70
motor planning 16
muscular dystrophy 22

nystagmus 9

osteogenesis imperfecta 24

page set-up 74–75
pain, insensibility to 11
parents and word processing 35–38
perception 11–12
perceptuo-motor difficulties 12
personality *see* motivation
physical considerations 65–66
practice sessions 77
printers 57–59
   accessibility 57
   compatibility with other equipment
     59
   portability 58–59
proprioception 10

recording on paper 7
rests for arms or wrists 48–49

scleroderma 23
sitting position 73

spina bifida 11
stability 28–29
syndactylism 24

teaching methods 72–73
tremor 20–21
   benign essential 20–21

upper case letters 78–79

vertical teaching method 4
visual acuity 8–10, 33
visual display unit *see* monitor
visual fields 9, 33, 55

wedge, foam rubber 19
word processing programmes 60
word processing skills 63–64
   and educational levels 34
   using in school 71–72
wrist rests *see* rests for arms or wrists